C000124811

christian verse
for meditation

WILLIAM STANLEY LOVELL

Copyright © 2006 William Stanley Lovell

First published in the United Kingdom in 2006

All rights reserved. No part of this publication may be reproduced, stored in a retrieval system or transmitted in any form or by any means, without the written permission of the publisher, nor be otherwise circulated in any form of binding or cover other than that in which it is published and without a similar condition being imposed on the subsequent purchaser.

A record of this book is available from the British Library.

ISBN 0-9552123-0-8 978-0-9552123-0-7

Published by William Stanley Lovell Burford Lodge Dorking Surrey RH5 6BP

THE STORY BEHIND THESE POEMS

*Christian poetry has been described as the "language of Eden".
William Cowper, one of England's greatest Christian poets and
hymn writers, believed that the language of Eden, before the fall
of man, was poetic language of great beauty.
He believed that we can see traces of that in the poetic scriptures
of the Old Testament.*

*Without doubt, poetry appeals very readily to the human mind
and lends itself to being memorised by the youngest reader.*

*In publishing these poems the purpose is to glorify God by
extolling His love and grace in Creation, Providence and
Redemption, to strengthen faith and point to a gracious God
whose love and care will meet the deepest need of every heart.*

*The gospel is "good news" for it tells us that Jesus has taken our
sins and suffered the judgment in our place so that we can be
forgiven and accepted with God. May these poems speak to many
people of the love of the Saviour who died for us and rose again.*

*Only He can satisfy the deep longings that lay in the human
heart and for which men and women so often fruitlessly search.
May He reveal Himself and encourage you to begin reading
the Bible where you will discover more of the wonders of
His love and grace.*

William Stanley Lovell

CONTENTS

The Creator's Love to Men   2

The Love of God   4
The Height and Depth of Love   6
Creation's Song   8
Creation's Story   10
Creation Made New   12
The Throne of God   14
In Praise of God   16
The Mighty God   18
The Sapphire Throne   20
Paradise Lost and Regained   22

God's Loving Kindness   26

God's Free Grace to Men   28
God's Everlasting Mercy   30
Gratitude   32
Unconditional Love   34
God's Mercy   36
Thanksgiving   38
The Father's Heart   40
A Gift of Love   42
Sovereign Love   44
Grace   46
The Shepherd God   48
Redemption's History   50

God's Protection   52

A Place of Safety   54
God's Keeping Power   56
Our Shelter   58
An Evening Prayer   60
My Needless Fear   62
Ministering Angels   64
Rejoicing in God   66
The King of all the Earth   68
A Rock and a Strong Tower   70

Jesus Our Saviour   72

The Name of Jesus   74
The True Vine   76
Jesus, Our Only Hope   78
All One in Christ   80
Jesus is Lord   82
The Sacrifice of Calvary   84
The Beauty of Jesus   86
The Love of Jesus   88
Immanuel   90
The Man Christ Jesus   92
Christmas   94
Gethsemane   96
Love Came Down   100
The Fairest Flower   102
The Door to Heaven   104
Who is this Man?   106

The Heart's Cry   108

The Voice   110
The Empty Place Within   112
A Prayer   114
Lifted Burdens   116
The Solitary Soul   118
A Young Man's Testimony   120
Peace   122
Fellowship   124

Faith & Hope   126

We Shall See God   128
The Happy Man   130
Resurrection Assured   132
Faith   134
The Saint's Rest   136
God Is My Friend   138
The Sinner's Hope   140
God's Eternal Purpose For Man   142
The Faith That Sees God   144
By Faith   146
A Birthday   148

THE CREATOR'S LOVE TO MEN

christian verse
for meditation

In this first section of Christian Verse for Meditation, the poetry seeks to extol the wonder of the Creator's love to men and women whom He has made in His image and after His likeness.

God, who created all things, has not left this world to itself, like a clock that has been wound up and then left alone by its maker. No, God is intimately concerned with every detail of His creation, from the smallest atom to the wheeling constellations of the heavens.

And the wonder of it all is that we are of His special interest and concern because He has created us to glorify Him and to enjoy His presence on this earth. Sadly, sin has come between us and God and caused a great separation that has blinded our eyes to His love and care for each soul that He has made.

We live in a world of sin and trouble. This is not how God created it but is the result of human rebellion against Him and His laws. Because of sin we no longer know God nor can have fellowship with Him.

However, it is through the work of Jesus Christ on the cross that fellowship is restored and we can again enter in to the wonders of His love and grace.

The awesomeness of God's majesty is only matched by the awesomeness of His great love to each individual soul, as evidenced by the sacrifice of Jesus for our sins.

And the Christian believer knows that the day is coming soon when Jesus will return to the earth to restore it to the beauty and perfection that God intended, and sin and the curse will be no more.

This poetry seeks to capture the greatness of God, who is Creator and Lord of all, yet who condescends to each person by desiring their love and friendship.

The Supreme Creator, the august Mover of the universe, listens to each man and woman who is at prayer. He is the lover of our souls and the beginning of our hope.
This majestic and awesome Person has condescended to us by sending to us His own Son, Jesus Christ, to whom He invites every man and woman to come that they might receive the forgiveness of all their sins and have everlasting life.

"He heals the broken hearted and binds up their wounds. He determines the number of stars and calls them each by name. Great is our Lord, and mighty in power; His understanding has no limit"
Psalm 147:3-5

christian verse
for meditation

THE LOVE OF GOD

The One who moves the stars,
Who placed them in the sky,
Is He who listens to our prayers
And hears us when we cry.

The great Creator, too,
Loves every soul He's made;
He is the ground of all our hope,
Flies swiftly to our aid.

In love, to earth He came,
As prophets did foretell,
Born of a humble Hebrew maid
To rescue us from hell!

He died upon the cross,
Our sins to gladly bear,
In pain He suffered for our loss
And did our sorrows share.

The great Creator dies!
A mystery so deep,
That He who made the starry skies
In death should fall asleep!

Death could not lay its claim,
The Prince of Life arose!
Up from the grave He came,
To heaven resplendent goes!

Such love demands a choice,
A choice we all must make,
Will Jesus be our Lord and God
Or will we Him forsake?

Lost soul, the choice is yours,
'Tis life or death you choose,
The life of Jesus, life that soars,
Or death, and Jesus lose.

To really appreciate the extent of God's mercy to us we need to understand something of the terrible nature of the fall of man in the beginning. From Paradise to banishment, and then the awful effects of the curse which came upon the whole creation when man sinned, is the context in which to set God's love to sinful men and women. Unless God had been rich in mercy none of us would have ever been saved. The Bible tells us that God delights in mercy and these verses seek to capture something of the wonder of our redemption.

"But God, who is rich in mercy, for his great love wherewith he loved us, even when we were dead in sins, has made us alive together with Christ, (by grace are you saved). And has raised us up together in heavenly places in Christ Jesus." Ephesians 2:4,5

christian verse
for meditation

THE HEIGHT AND DEPTH OF LOVE

My God, how wonderful you are,
Your mercy, O so deep and large!
That saves the fallen sons of men,
And takes them to your heart again!

You sent your Son, th'eternal Word,
(Made flesh, to save a fallen world)
Who, in our place, embraced the cross,
Died there at such tremendous cost!

Oh awful fact, the fall of man!
That brought the curse, imposed the ban
From that fair garden, Paradise,
Where Satan blinded Adam's eyes.

The curse, it drove the first man out,
To wander, lost, in sin's dark cloud,
To sweat and toil, with tears and pain,
'Til One should open it's gates again.

The curse, it fell upon that One
Who took our place (it was God's Son),
Man's Surety now, who paid the price,
The Lamb of God, the sacrifice.

Rejoice, you men, and angels too,
For this, Messiah came to do!
Yes! God Himself would suffer shame
When man alone should bear the blame!

Good news is this to men of faith,
The curse removed, an act of grace!
None to condemn, whom God does bless,
Through Jesus' blood and righteousness!

Come then you men, and see the sight
Of Paradise in holy light!
It's gates flung wide, where glory shines
On Adam's sons, Messiah's bride.

So no more need of sun or moon,
Such radiance shines from Jesus' throne!
No heat, no cold, nor sorrow, nor pain,
Where God with all His saints does reign!

It has been said that God has two books through which He speaks to mankind. The Book of Creation and the Bible. The psalmist, in the verse quoted below, tells us that each day the creation speaks to all mankind of the Creator and His love. Furthermore, he emphasises the fact that the creation doesn't just speak to us but "pours forth speech"! What do you see when you look at the beauty of mountains, seas and skies? When you see the beauty of the flowers and trees that blossom and flourish in the warmth of sunshine after the barrenness of winter? Do you see God at work or have you never stopped to consider who might be the great Designer and Architect of it all? The psalmist had no doubt that the creation was fashioned and made by the great Creator God who has revealed Himself both in nature and in the Bible itself.

"The heavens declare the glory of God; the skies proclaim the work of His hands. Day after day they pour forth speech; night after night they display their knowledge. There is no speech or language where their voice is not heard. Their voice goes out into all the world."
Psalm 19:1-3

christian verse
for meditation

Bible references:
Job chapter 37
Romans 1:18-20

CREATION'S SONG

The earth declares God's awesome power,
In sea and sky, and tree and flower;
In every age their voice is heard,
Creation's song mens' hearts have stirred.

Throughout the earth, melodious cords,
The notes of praise to nature's Lord,
Go forth to men in every land,
Tell out the works of God's own hand.

How sad that some no song do hear,
No hymn of praise, no theme to cheer;
They blindly go their chosen way
And live their lives just for today.

But each new day, the song renewed,
Sings out the love of nature's Lord,
That all would stop and listen to
The song creation sings anew.

In an attempt to discredit the biblical record of creation men have introduced a theory of evolution which they claim is based on scientific facts. Nothing could be further from the truth. This is a pseudo-science which is based, not on scientific fact, but on an atheistic philosophy that attempts to get rid of God and so avoid the consequences of a future judgment. The wonder and beauty of creation, from the vast constellations of stars and planets to the smallest cell of which our bodies are made, all point to a God of infinite power and wisdom. Furthermore, the Bible tells us quite clearly that God created all things by Jesus Christ, who upholds all things by the word of His power. Your very existence, as well as the constellations of stars, are all dependent upon Jesus Christ, who has all power in heaven and on earth.

"And God said, Let us make man in our image, after our likeness.... So God created man in his own image, in the image of God created he him; male and female created he them.... And the Lord God formed man of the dust of the ground and breathed into his nostrils the breath of life; and man became a living soul."
Genesis 1:26,27 and 2:7

"Through faith we understand that the worlds were framed by the word of God, so that things which are seen were made of things which do appear." Hebrews 1:3

christian verse
for meditation

CREATION'S STORY

Before the world was formed for man
Or countless stars with all their host,
The Triune God, in glory dwelt,
The Father, Son and Holy Ghost.

These three Persons, bless'd Three in One,
Uncreated, needing none!
Adored and loved in union sweet,
Would share their love they felt was meet.

Let us make man, they then agreed,
In our own image, a holy seed,
Our likeness in a race of men
Upon the earth, the gate of heaven.

From dust of earth, created him,
A living soul, unmarred by sin,
In His own image both were made,
The man and woman in Eden's glade.

The world, as formed by God's own hand,
A heaven on earth, Immanuel's land;
A paradise for man to enjoy,
And joyful days for his employ.

How good is God, our dearest Friend,
Who plans our good and pleasures send,
How much we have, yet sends us more!
Our God and Maker we adore.

God created all things for His own pleasure. But He always had in mind the creation of man to enjoy with Him all the beauties that we see in nature. And the purpose of creation is for the glory of God. In the scriptures we see even creation itself bursting into song before us as we worship our creator God. What a wonderful picture of joy these words of Isaiah give us!

"You will go out in joy and be led forth in peace; the mountains and the hills will burst into song before you, and all the trees of the field will clap their hands." Isaiah 55:12

christian verse
for meditation

Bible references:
1 Corinthians 15:12-28
2 Peter 3:1-13
Revelation 21:1-4

CREATION MADE NEW

The hills and valleys sing for joy,
Trees of the field, they clap their hands,
All nature sings to Him above
Whose wisdom this creation planned.

The heavens declare His marvellous Name,
The earth, His skill in every place;
All nature fair tells of His fame,
His wisdom, power, His love and grace.

How great is He who did conceive
Such wondrous works for man to enjoy;
What love is this that gave to all
A perfect world for their employ?

How much we owe to such a God,
Who planned such bliss for us down here!
How sad that we have rudely trod
Upon such works of love and care.

But Jesus came to make anew
The world which man had ruined so;
He will return and then will show,
A world restored down here below.

Hills and valleys will sing for joy,
The trees themselves will clap their hands!
And men and angels all employ
Their voices in resounding praise!

Jesus is God who became man. This is the incarnation, that we celebrate at Christmas. But he came into this world for a purpose, to pay the price for human sin. He is the Lamb of God. He is called the Lamb of God because in ancient Jewish worship a lamb was sacrificed as a sin offering. That lamb could not remove the sins of the people but it told them that Someone would come who could and would, even Jesus.

He died for our sins but he is now risen and is seated on the throne of the universe as King. In the book of Revelation we are given a picture of that throne and to our wonder we see that all who have trusted Jesus are with him around that throne.

"Therefore they are before the throne of God and serve Him day and night in His temple and He who sits on the throne will spread His tent over them. Never again will they hunger; never again will they thirst." Revelation 7:15,16

christian verse
for meditation

Bible references:
Psalm 47
Isaiah 6:1-5
John 1:29-34
Hebrews 4:14-16

THE THRONE OF GOD

Unseen by eyes of mortal men
There stands the Throne of God.
High in the heavens beyond our ken
Where mortals never trod.

Who sits upon that Throne on high?
What is His Name, I pray?
It is the Lamb who once did die
For sin, it's price to pay.

The Lamb upon the Throne now reigns,
A sceptre in His hand;
And all the world will own that Name
And bow to His command.

Around that throne the angels throng,
To worship and adore,
"Worthy is the Lamb", their song,
Who died for men on earth.

There stands the Lamb, in glory now,
With eyes a flaming fire,
His head now crowned with many crowns,
Adored by angel choirs.

Though wondrous is this heavenly scene,
More wonders are to come!
For mortal men, from sin made clean,
Will join the angelic throng!

Yes, men and angels will unite!
And sing around that Throne;
These are the men with robes made white,
For whom the Lamb was slain.

Ten thousand times ten thousand, sing
"O worthy is the Lamb!"
Myriads throng that blessed scene,
All joining hand in hand.

Yes, men redeemed, and angels bright,
With glory shining round!
Mercy and truth will then unite,
To make all joys abound!

So let us join the heavenly throng
With songs on earth today,
And tune our hearts to sing their song
Until the break of day.

And then shall every tear be dry,
And every pain be gone,
As angels take us up on high
And lead us to the Lamb.

Psalm 148 is one of the hallelujah psalms in which we
find all creation praising God who made all things for
His own glory. These verses seek to capture something
of that theme and to remind us that it is our privilege, as well as
our duty, to praise and thank God for all things that He has made.

"Praise the Lord!
Praise the Lord from the heavens; praise Him in the heights!
Praise Him, all his angels; praise Him, all this host!
Praise Him, sun and moon; praise Him all you shining stars!
Praise Him, you highest heavens, and you waters about
the heavens!
Let them praise the Name of the Lord, for He commanded
and they were created!" Psalm 148. 1-5

christian verse
for meditation

Bible references:
Psalm 8
Matthew 21:14-16

IN PRAISE OF GOD

In heaven, the angels sing God's praise;
Sun, moon and stars His power.
On earth, the saints their voices raise
Their songs from hour to hour.

Fire, hail and snow, at His command,
Fulfil His mighty word:
That nature's Lord, in every land,
Be everywhere adored.

The mountains and the hills around,
The trees and cattle too.
All speak of Him, their voices sound,
Declaring God is true.

Kings of the earth, join in this song,
And men and children too;
Let every creature join the throng,
And praise; which is His due.

If all nature sings God's praise,
Should men have silent tongues?
If sun, moon, stars their voices raise,
Should men be counted dumb?

Come, praise the Lord, who sits above,
Whose glory is on high;
And He will bless, and prove His love
To all who will draw nigh.

The most astounding fact of history is that God became man. He did not cease to be God but in the Person of Jesus Christ He took our human nature and became a man too. He is the God-man, who, as man, died for our sins.

"For unto us a child is born, to us a son is given, and the government will be upon His shoulders. And He will be called Wonderful Counsellor, Mighty God, Everlasting Father, Prince of Peace. Of the increase of His government there will be no end". Isaiah 9:6,7

christian verse
for meditation

Bible references:
John 18:28-40
John 19:1-16
Acts 1:1-11

THE MIGHTY GOD

Exalted above all is Jesus our King.
Come ye redeemed His praises to sing.
Lift your hands up on high,
let your hearts swell with praise
And give Him the glory,
the Ancient of Days!

Wonderful, Counsellor,
Mighty God is His Name,
He rules in the heavens,
eternal the same;
His presence on earth
He delights to impart,
Descending in grace,
possessing our hearts.

How gracious this King,
who to sinners will come,
Their hearts will He change,
a throne to become!
This Saviour is Jesus, 'twas for us
that He died,
Risen, ascended at His own Father's side.

In triumph He reigns over angels and men.
Thrones upon earth as well as in heaven;
His saints up above, and those
still on earth,
Delight to adore and praise
Him with mirth.

In the Old Testament we find that some of the prophets were given extraordinary visions of heaven and the throne of God. Ezekiel is a case in point. He was a young man and had been taken captive with the Jewish people and transported to Babylon. Whilst there he was given a vision of the throne of God, and he saw that it had the appearance of sapphire. He saw Someone on the throne who was so glorious that he fell on his face before him. The One he saw was the Son of God. He was given this vision by way of encouragement and so that he could inspire his fellow captives in the midst of a heathen culture. The following verses try to capture something of his vision and show that on the throne of heaven is the One who loved us and died for us, even Jesus.

"Above the expanse, over their heads, was what looked like a throne of sapphire, and high above on the throne was a figure like that of a man.....and brilliant light surrounded him" Ezekiel 1:26-28

christian verse
for meditation

THE SAPPHIRE THRONE

A stranger in a foreign land
Amidst the heathen, lone did stand,
But God, his God, a vision gave,
That filled his sight with awesome blaze!

The prophet saw that blessed One
In burning fire upon the Throne,
He saw His likeness, as a man,
And prostrate fell before that Sun!

See, in the Throne our Surety stands,
See, the nail marks in His hands!
And see that face, once spat upon,
Now radiant, brighter than the sun!

Jesus, the brightness of that Throne,
(For all our sins He did atone),
The Eternal God, He rules supreme,
And intercedes our cause to plead.

Before that aweful Throne so bright,
You, too, may come and see that sight:
Adore and worship at His feet
The One who waits, our souls to greet.

These verses span the whole of the work of creation and man's place in it. The magnificence and the glory of the eternal plan, and especially the exalted place that man was to have in it, as God's regent, to rule and look after it, is far above what we now see or ever have seen, or indeed, can imagine. All that glory vanished immediately Adam sinned against the known will of God.

The fall of man, which is his rebellion against his Maker, brought the curse upon the whole creation and with it came death. The original must have been of unsurpassed beauty for He who made it, who Himself is perfect, pronounced it all to be very good.

But what was lost by the first Adam will be regained by the second Adam, who is Jesus Christ. In His death for sin, and in taking the curse upon Himself on the cross, He opened the way for the regeneration of all creation. There will be a new heavens and a new earth wherein dwells righteousness. The Bible puts it like this in Romans 8:21 - "the whole creation itself will be set free from its bondage to decay and obtain the glorious liberty of the children of God."

Through faith in Jesus Christ we ourselves will be regenerated by what Jesus himself described as the "new birth", without which we shall never enjoy that future state of bliss which will shortly be ushered in at the return of Jesus Christ to this world.

Jesus said, "Except a man be born again, he cannot see the kingdom of God." John 3:3

christian verse
for meditation

PARADISE LOST AND REGAINED

In endless ages, or e'er time was,
Before the stars their courses ran,
Or sun and moon shone down upon
This earthly scene designed for man;
There, in eternity, aweful infinity,
The Triune God, the Three in One,
In bliss unknown to mortal man,
There, planned creation's form;
And man, in His own image drawn,
To reign as king o'er all that work
God's hand would make!

In primal beauty, unmarred by sin,
This man, in moral likeness made,
Unto his God and image true,
To rule the earth and to subdue
All things his Maker had designed.
Unrivalled bliss for all mankind
Was His intent and purpose bent,
In love unbounded, without a shore,
To enjoy his God for evermore
So God did plan!

In moral beauty, man did stand
There with his God, at His right hand!
With all creation at his feet,
To rule as king, for it was meet
That man, as regent, for his God
Should tend and care creation's form,
So wisely made by th'Eternal Word;
Who called the stars and moon and sun
To shine their light on earth's fair form,
For man to enjoy!

In Paradise our parents walked,
Sublime in innocence (now unknown)
Before the Tempter stole their crown,
Usurped God's rights, their fall ensured,
And ruined all that God had planned
For all the race (now to be damned)
To enjoy creation's vistas fair,
And heaven's smile for all to share.
Too late, the judgment fell, severe;
And man there died!

A ruined world, a fallen race,
A cursed ground, and thorns in place
Of primal beauty God had wrought,
Was now man's lot: and tears, and toil,
And pain, to break the unyielding soil.
But more! His God would walk no more
With this man, as once before,
In evening cool, at close of day.
No, in that cursed place
God would not stay!

Is there no hope for ruined man,
And ruined earth, now clothed in thorns,
With enmity and strife now born?
Can fallen man retrieve his loss?
Ah, no! A second Adam with His cross,
Must take man's part and bear the curse!
Into a ruined world so entered One,
The Son of man, God's only Son,
To bear the curse upon the tree,
And set man free!

Continued

christian verse
for meditation

PARADISE LOST AND REGAINED
CONTINUED

This Son of man, the Eternal Word,
By whom were made the stars and sun,
Entered this world which He had made,
To bear the curse and set man free
From sin's cruel chain and tyranny.
In Adam's place He took His stand
And bore our sin; this He had planned
E'er time was, or worlds did frame,
This Man, who to our rescue came,
Died on the tree!

It was for love of humankind
That God's own Son, for us to find,
Came down from heav'n to seek the lost
And pay the price at awful cost.
But down He came and did His work
Triumphed o'er sin and Satan's worst,
He rose again and left the grave
And so His people He did save.
The curse removed, His work complete
To heaven He goes and takes His seat,
At God's right hand!

In glory now, upon the Throne,
Creation's Lord, His work quite done,
Calls to His saints to lift their eyes,
And wait for Him, who from the skies
Will come again with angel hosts,
Restore to man what Adam lost;
This world a Paradise remake
For man, redeemed, his place to take:
No sin, no death, no tears to shed,
The curse removed, in bliss to dwell,
As God had planned!

GOD'S LOVING KINDNESS

*In this second section the poetry invites the reader to rejoice in
God's loving kindness towards us.*

*God's free grace and His mercy are the expressions of His love
and concern for us, both for time and for eternity. God's grace is
His free and unmerited favour to undeserving men and women.*

*Imperfection is the leading characteristic of our human race.
It was not always so. The Bible speaks of us as being "fallen"
which simply means that our first parents, Adam and Eve, fell
from the state of perfection in which they were created.
They were guilty of original sin against the revealed will of God
their Creator.*

*We are sinners, too, both by inheritance from our first parents
and also in practice. It is against this background that the grace of
God shines out in all its wonder. Instead of rejecting us God sent
His Son to bear our sin and thus make us fit for heaven.*

*These poems, which are all based on scripture, reveal something
of the character and nature of God. Whilst His face is set against
sin in all its forms He nonetheless so loves the sinner that,
in the Person of Jesus Christ, He suffered the penalty of our
sin in our behalf.*

*Here we see a loving heavenly Father's heart revealed in all its
compassion and mercy. A Father who longs to have us walk with
Him and enjoy fellowship with Him.*

*May these poems open your heart to taste and see that the Lord
is good to all that put their trust in Him.*

One of the most amazing truths that we find in the Bible is that, though we are sinners, God so loved us that He sent His one and only Son, Jesus, into this world to be our Saviour. Equally amazing is that whilst God has chosen to save men and women who put their trust in Jesus, the angels who sinned and became devils He has not chosen to save, but has reserved them for judgment and eternal punishment. How blessed we are that God should show we men and women such mercy! This truth is found in the Bible in Hebrews chapter 2 and verses 16-17.

"For surely it is not angels God helps, but Abraham's descendants (all men and women who believe). For this reason He (Jesus) had to be made like to His brothers in every way, in order that He might become a merciful high priest in service to God and that He might make atonement for the sins of the people."

christian verse
for meditation

Bible references:
Romans 3:9-26
Ephesians 2:1-10

GOD'S FREE GRACE TO MEN

From heaven the sinning angels fell,
And wrath and darkness chained them down;
Then man, poor man, he sinned as well
But mercy lifts him to a crown!

Amazing work of God's free grace
That pours such love upon our race!
For rebel man who stands so proud
Has sins as dark as any cloud.

But God in mercy sent His Son,
His only, well-beloved One,
And in our place our guilt He took
Condemned for us, sins fetters broke.

What love is this that He should die,
And guilty sinners lifted high?
No more condemned, absolved from sin,
And heaven's prize for us to win.

Amazing grace, this love of God,
Who leads us on where He has trod,
To put our trust in Him alone,
Who takes us to our Father's home.

Psalm 103 challenges us to lift up our hearts and praise our great God and Saviour for His everlasting mercy. The writer of the Psalm, King David, was full of how much that God had done for him. This theme is timeless for everyone who has come to love the Saviour and who can echo these same sentiments.

For the Christian, it is his joy to praise God for removing his sins and transgressions. God's mercy, the Bible tells us, is higher than the heavens and His kindness like a great deep. Let us constantly remind ourselves of this wonderful truth and ever show our gratitude by loving and serving Him in return.

"For the Lord your God is a merciful God....". Deuteronomy 4:31
"The Lord is full of compassion and mercy." James 5:11

christian verse
for meditation

Bible references:
Romans 3:9-26
Ephesians 2:1-10

GOD'S EVERLASTING MERCY

O thou my soul bless God the Lord
For all His mercies to me;
My sins He surely does forgive
And loves me, oh so freely!

Forget not all His benefits,
That are so freely given,
He heals me from my sicknesses
And saves me from destruction.

My life He crowns with kindnesses,
And satisfies with goodness,
My youth He does renew again,
With strength He daily blesses.

How merciful and gracious is
The God of our salvation,
So slow to anger, full of grace,
His mercy like a fountain.

He will not always chide with us,
Nor does He keep His anger,
He knows that we are made of dust,
And loves us as a Father.

Our sins, He's not rewarded us
According to their merit,
But in His love, though He be just,
Removes them without limit.

As far as east is from the west,
Our transgressions has removéd,
In depths of sea they have been cast
And cannot be retrievéd.

This mercy of the Lord our God
Is mercy everlasting!
To all of those who fear His name
On Whom their hope is casting.

Ingratitude is something that we deplore. To be unthankful for gifts received, or kindnesses shown, is a sad commentary on us. Perhaps we have never been conscious of our ingratitude to God for all the benefits that we have received from His hand. The prophet Isaiah, who was both a prophet and of royal descent, reminds us of our need to thank and praise God for all that He has done for us.

"I will tell of the kindness of the Lord, the deeds for which He is to be praised, according to all that the Lord has done for us - yes, the many good things He has done......" Isaiah 63:7

christian verse
for meditation

Bible references:
Matthew 7:7-12
Romans 11:33-36

GRATITUDE

Put all your trust in God,
Make Him your strength and song,
Let everlasting praise be yours
For all that He has done.

What yet He'll do for you
Your heart can ne'er conceive,
Beyond your ken and wildest dreams
Your hopes He will fulfil.

The Mighty God is He
Who watches over you,
To bless you with His perfect love,
And show you He is true.

What love is this, so free?
That comes, a gift of grace,
From God who made us for Himself,
Whose Son died in our place.

We are His chosen ones,
For whom He died alone,
So that to heaven we soon may come
And share the Father's home.

What is love? This is the great question that philosophers, poets and romantics have tried to answer over the centuries. Love is a gift from God. All human love is a spark from the great Flame of Love which is God, for God is Love. Uniquely, His love is unconditional love. It is a love that is not dependent on anything attractive in us. He loves us because He loves us!. God's love is seen supremely in Jesus dying for us on the cross. It was love that prayed on the cross, "Father, forgive them for they know not what they do." There is no one beyond the reach of God's love because it is free and unconditional.

christian verse
for meditation

Bible references:
John 3:16-18
1 John 4:7-12

UNCONDITIONAL LOVE

In heaven or earth, or sea or sky,
Can love so pure and free be found?
A love that asks not for return
But loves because by love is bound
To seek the loved one's best?

Is there such love that only gives?
And gives, because it's nature is
To share it's fullness like a stream,
That flows from sources infinite:
A boundless spring of life?

The soul, it craves to know such love,
And asks, Can it be found?
Yes, look above beyond this world,
To One whose Name Himself is Love,
Whose love to all abounds.

This pure love came down from heaven,
In mortal flesh appeared!
And by His Spirit gives Himself,
A flowing stream of endless life,
A living fount within.

This heaven-sent love, so boundless, free,
A Father's heart displays,
And changes all our hearts that we,
Now bound by those same cords of love,
Will love and be as free.

God's mercy is beyond measure. It is higher than the heavens. It is deeper than the deepest sea. His mercy is His love in action to help us in our helplessness. The psalmist captured this thought in these beautiful words.

"Your love, O Lord, reaches to the heavens, your faithfulness to the skies. Your righteousness is like the mighty mountains, your justice like the great deep. O Lord, you preserve man and beast. How priceless is your unfailing love! Both high and low among men find refuge in the shadow of your wings."
Psalm 36:5-7

christian verse
for meditation

Bible references:
Exodus 20:1-6
Exodus 34: 5-7
Nehemiah 9:28-31

GOD'S MERCY

God's mercy reaches to the heavens,
His faithfulness, the clouds:
Such love, beyond mere human sense,
God has, in Christ, revealed.

How excellent, your kindness, Lord,
How bountiful and free!
By all your saints you are adored,
O blessed Trinity.

What radiance shines out from your Throne!
Where angels shield their eyes:
Such uncreated beauty shown
To saints, their glittering prize!

Who, on such glories, dares to look,
On all-consuming light?
The men of faith, washed in the blood,
Their stains made clean and white!

Whose blood is this, that can make clean
Such stains and guilt of sin?
'Tis Jesus' blood, and His alone,
That cleanses hearts within.

So now, by faith, the saints behold
A Father's smiling face,
And to the ends of all the world
Tell forth His saving grace.

This 21st century is characterised by so many pressures upon people, both young and old alike. The consequence is seen in stress-related sickness and the increased demand for sedatives and sleeping pills by large numbers of people. God has given us His answer as to how to lead a stress-free life. It is to put one's trust in Him who cares for us and who provides all that we need in this life and for eternity. Jesus asks the question, Can you, by worrying, add one hour to your life? And then He draws our attention to the birds and flowers which He cares and provides for, telling us that we are far more important than they are, therefore will He not also provide for us too? God is a prayer-hearing God. Sadly, and all too often, we seek answers to our problems from anywhere but from the Saviour who patiently waits for us to come to Him and who has all power and wisdom to deal with them on our behalf.

"Do not be anxious about anything, but in everything, by prayer and petition, with thanksgiving, present your requests to God. And the peace of God, which transcends all understanding, will guard your hearts and minds in Christ Jesus ". Philippians 4:6,7

christian verse
for meditation

THANKSGIVING

O Lord my God, who hears my prayer,
I thank You for your love and care:
Not once, nor twice, but every day
You bend your ear and hear me pray.

What love is this, that One so great,
Should stoop so low and on me wait?
But Love divine will find a way
To bless and keep me day by day.

I am your child and love You so,
For You have loved me, one so low:
What comfort, this, that God so great
Should hear my prayer and on me wait!

Great God, what can I do for You?
For You who makes our lives anew,
My love is all that You desire,
So make my heart a flaming fire.

A fire of love, ablaze with heaven,
A love no sin can ever leaven,
That I may love You more and more,
And have in heaven a treasure store.

God's love for us is even more profound than the love of a mother for her new-born child! The mother's love for her child is a love implanted in her heart by this God who is our Father. It is a reflection of His love, a love which is overwhelming in its gentleness and greatness. Although God is almighty, yet His love for us is as tender and gentle as a mother's for her new-born child. And He tells us to cast all our care upon Him because He cares for us. With such a God we have nothing to fear, neither poverty, sickness nor being forsaken. A babe in arms doesn't worry about anything but simply rests in its mother's care and love. God calls us into such a relationship with Himself, day by day.

"Though my father and mother forsake me,
the Lord will receive me." Psalm 27:10
"A Father to the fatherless, a defender of widows,
is God in His holy dwelling." Psalm 68:5

christian verse
for meditation

Bible references:
Isaiah 40:11
John 14:15,16

THE FATHER'S HEART

A word from God fell in my ear,
It spoke of love, and banished fear;
A Father's heart that seeks our love
And calls us to the realms above!

Our hearts then soar to worlds unknown
Where mansions wait for all His own;
And at the door our Father waits
To welcome home His faithful saints!

And so we pray and sing His praise
Who loves us from eternal days,
Who sent His Son to make us free
And touch our hearts so joyously.

To God our Saviour all praise is due
Whose faithful love is ever new,
Who shed His blood and took our sin,
Opened heaven's gate to let us in.

Praise God from whom all blessings flow,
Praise Him you people here below,
Praise Him above you angel host,
Praise Father, Son and Holy Ghost.

"For God so loved the world that He gave His one and only Son, that whoever believes in him should not perish but have everlasting life."
John 3:16

This is perhaps one of the best-known verses in the Bible. It encapsulates some of the greatest truths in the scriptures and demonstrates the amazing love of a holy God towards sinful men and women. Here is grace in action. The love of God put forth in incomparable measure by His giving of His only Son to suffer and to die in order to save us. If we are not amazed by this then it is questionable whether we are truly Christian. What more could God have done? What greater treasure could He have given than the One who is the Son of His love?

christian verse
for meditation

Bible references:
Matthew 11:25-30
Matthew 23:37-39

A GIFT OF LOVE

What love is this, that God so loved,
To give His only Son?
And on the cross to shed His blood:
That work now fully done!

What stoop was this, that Jesus made?
So lowly and so kind!
Who loved us all, for whom He prayed,
And came, for us to find.

What tenderness thus fills God's heart,
And yearns for His lost sons!
Today, He still calls tenderly-
Repent, my child, and come!

Such love! But ruined by the fall,
Men, hardened, turn away,
Resist the gospel's gracious call,
And cry, "another day!"

But will there be another day?
And will God call again?
Salvation missed, whilst still today,
May never be reclaimed.

Why will you turn away from Love?
This Jesus cares for you!
And longs to send the heavenly Dove
To guide you into truth.

So come to this dear Friend today,
And put your trust in Him,
His promise is to ever stay
And give you peace within.

One of the most amazing facts of the gospel is that God does not wait for men and women to reform themselves before He accepts them, but invites them to come to Him just as they are. These verses express something of the amazement of the believer at this act of free grace on the part of a holy God for unholy men and women. "But God commends His love towards us, in that, while we were yet sinners, Christ died for us." Romans 5:8

Bible references:
John 15:9-17
John 17:20-26
Romans 5:1-11

SOVEREIGN LOVE

Dear Lord, how can it be
That You should have such love for me?
What was it that, in love, You saw
In one so sinful and so poor?

'Twas not for any good in us,
He came to men made of the dust;
'Twas only love that brought Him here,
For souls of men He counted dear.

From Your exalted throne on high,
On wings of love, did quickly fly,
To seek and save that which was lost
With such delight, and spurned the cost!

See, you sinners, your Maker dies!
Yes, He who lives above the skies,
For you, for you, He died alone
On Calvary's cross, there to atone.

And this was all for sinners poor,
Who knew You not, and looked not for
Their Maker who desired their love;
Which brought Him from His throne above.

Is it nought to you who pass Him by,
The One whom they did crucify;
Who shed His blood to cleanse your sin,
Opened heaven's gate to let you in?

What love is this, our Maker has,
For souls of men whose lot is cast
In paths of sin and enmity,
'Gainst Him who made us sons to be.

Come quickly now, be reconciled
To God your Maker, undefiled,
With all your sins washed clean away
To walk with Jesus day by day.

45

We often use the word "grace" but are we aware of the wonderful meaning when we speak of God's grace? It means the free, unmerited, favour of God. God freely forgiving our sins without any payment by us. It means God choosing to shower His love on us in spite of all our faults and failings. He loves us because He loves us. That is grace. You cannot buy God's favour, you cannot earn it or inherit it from your parents, it is freely given - without price! And it is free to all men and women on earth, whoever they are or however low they may have sunk into iniquity. It is grace that saves a man from the depths of despair and it is grace that makes him a new man in Christ. And it is grace that enables him to reach heaven!

"For it is by grace you have been saved, though faith, and this is not from yourselves, it is the gift of God, not by works, so that no one can boast." Ephesians 2:8

christian verse
for meditation

Bible references:
Romans 3:21-26

GRACE

God called me by his grace,
Revealed his Son in me,
And showed to me his smiling face
And gave me eyes to see!

What is this grace so free,
Bestowed by God on man?
A gift of love, that all may see
The Way that leads to heaven!

How wonderful the grace
That God thus shows to men,
A grace that has no boundaries
As free, as high, as heaven!

Such grace, just freely take,
That God holds out to you!
Do not despise nor love forsake
Grace, like the morning dew.

To God give all the praise,
To him be blessings given;
Let us adore him all our days,
Who leads us home to heaven!

The prophet Isaiah describes to us something of the nature and character of Almighty God. He has been speaking of His greatness and then contrasts this with His gentleness and care for the weak and needy. These lovely words are found in Isaiah 40:11.

"He tends His flock like a shepherd: He gathers the lambs in His arms and carries them close to His heart; he gently leads those that have young."

THE SHEPHERD GOD

With shepherd's heart our God on high,
Enthroned in glory in the sky.
He feeds His flock as shepherds do,
With gentle hand both strong and true.

The lambs He gathers with His arm,
And carries them to keep from harm,
He gently leads all those with young,
To bring them safely to His home.

But pause awhile, who is this God?
So great in wisdom and in power,
Who stoops in love to you and me,
To bless and keep from hour to hour?

The stars in heavens, He tells each one,
Their names He knows, He put them there!
This mighty God with arm so strong,
Who keeps His flock and hears our prayer.

He heals the men with broken hearts,
And bindeth up their wounds so sore,
This God who telleth all the stars,
Lifts up the meek and goes before.

He measures heaven with a span,
And weighs the mountains in His scales;
Increases strength to those who faint,
Gives eagles wings to those who wait!

Have you not known, have you not heard?
Creation's Lord, th'eternal God,
So strong in power and wisdom too,
He cannot faint nor weary grow.

Behold with me this glorious God,
This King who sits enthroned on high,
He is the Lord who bore your sins
And died to bring poor sinners nigh.

Bow down to Him, this glorious Lord,
Come worship Him, let all adore,
Angels and men your voices raise,
And sing your great Creator's praise.

The meaning of the word "redemption" is to buy back something that was lost, and has become someone else's possession.

When man sinned he forfeited his relationship to God who created him - so coming under the dominion of Satan.

The only way back to a restored relationship with God is for the "redemption price" to be paid.

The "redemption price" is the blood of Jesus Christ, God's Son, which he shed on the cross for all mankind.

"You were not redeemed with corruptible things such as silver and gold... but with the precious blood of Christ, as of a lamb without blemish and without spot." 1 Peter 1:18, 19

christian verse
for meditation

REDEMPTION'S HISTORY

When Adam sinned and brought
God's curse,
All nature sighed and wept:
From Eden's garden both went forth,
In tears and unbelief.

Sad day that saw such grief and loss,
When angels wept on high!
That man should heed the Tempter's voice
And so believe a lie!

And yet the stage was being set
For God's display of grace,
In His eternal purposes
Redeeming Adam's race.

To Adam was the promise given,
A Seed to bruise the foe,
His one and only Son from heaven
Would come to suffer woe.

What love was this that pitied man,
Who heeded Satan's voice?
And left his God whose gracious plan
Was bliss for all his race.

But now we see God's heart of love
Unfolded at the cross;
And angels stoop in wondering gaze
As Jesus suffered loss.

Upon the cross He bore our sins,
There, God proclaimed His grace,
Declaring to a fallen world
That Jesus took our place.

And now, dear friend, does Jesus' love
Mean anything to you?
That God so loved, to give His Son
To make your life anew?

New hearts, new lives, that is His work,
Hearts broken He'll restore;
Just call on Him and plead His name,
His grace on you He'll pour.

GOD'S PROTECTION

christian verse
for meditation

In this third section the poetry has the theme of God's protection of His people.

God, who is eternal, and infinite in power and wisdom, is more than sufficient for all the needs of all of His people. The Bible tells us that He neither slumbers nor sleeps. It also declares that His arm is not shortened that it cannot save.

In other words, God's power and love are such that all His believing people can rest in the quiet assurance that He takes care of us day by day.

Furthermore, He also sends His angels to watch over us. These heavenly beings are His messengers and are sent to minister to us and to help us in our trials. Though unseen, they are always present.

The Christian believer is not exempt from the trials and tribulations that come to all men and women at different times in their lives. These trials are meant to bring us closer to God and discover that He is able to hold us up and cause us to stand strong and to rejoice, whatever may be our lot in this world, confident in the knowledge that He works all things together for our eternal good.

"The Name of the Lord is a strong tower, the righteous run into it and are safe!" Proverbs 18:10

We live in an uncertain world. A world of sudden calamities and dangers. A world that is becoming increasingly violent and frightening. The Christian believer has the assurance that he is under divine protection, that God is his shelter and that nothing will happen to him except by God's permission. Even then, God will make all things work together for the good of His children. This is what the psalmist assures us of in Psalm 91.

"He who dwells in the shelter of the Most High will rest in the shadow of the Almighty." Psalm 91:1

christian verse
for meditation

Bible references:
Romans 8:28-39
Hebrews 6:13-20

A PLACE OF SAFETY

A refuge and a hiding place
Is God, most high, to me;
From harm and from all violence
He guards and keeps me free.

His shadow keeps my soul at rest
In quiet confidence,
For God, the Lord, in whom I trust,
Is my secure defence.

His feathers are my covering,
A refuge are His wings;
He spreads them over all who trust:
From danger safely brings.

No evil can befall the man
Who hides beneath His wing;
No plague nor darkness can disturb,
Nor evil tidings bring.

God's promise is to set on high
The man who knows His Name;
To honour and to satisfy,
And take away all shame.

So let us praise our God so great,
Join heavenly choirs above;
Let all the earth extol His Name,
Our Jesus, King of Love.

*These verses were written for an elderly Christian who was troubled
by many fears at night time. Often she would sit in her chair
because she was too afraid to go to bed. These verses brought this
lady great comfort and consolation. And it is the same God who
watches over all His people to protect and keep them from all evil.
He is the God who neither slumbers nor sleeps but is ever watchful
and caring for all who commit themselves to Him.*

"For so He giveth His beloved sleep" Psalm 127.2

GOD'S KEEPING POWER

The Lord your keeper is by day,
His watchful eye ne'er closes,
And through the night His angels bright
Their presence interposes.

So, dear friend, both day and night
Rest in His loving kindness,
And be at peace for in His sight
His care for you addresses.

Though days be dark, and all seems wrong,
Your God will ne'er forsake you,
But will draw near and give a song
To cheer and so to bless you.

Our Jesus knows the way you take,
He lived on earth before you,
And all He did was for your sake
To save and to preserve you.

One of the comforting things about God is that He is concerned always for our well-being and our protection from physical as well as from spiritual dangers. He is the Almighty God who will move heaven and earth in defence of His children. Believers are the "apple of His eye". Troubles do come to us but, just as surely, God will always bring good out of them, as He promised - "All things work together for good to those that love God."

"He will shield you with His wings! They will shelter you. His faithful promises are your armour." Psalm 91:4

christian verse
for meditation

Bible references:
Matthew 8:23-27
Romans 8:31-39
Ephesians 6:10-18

OUR SHELTER

Under His wings we can shelter secure:
Safe in the knowledge His love is so sure,
Under His wings, we can rest without fear,
For Jesus has said "I will always be near".

When storms fill our sky, and darkness surrounds,
When hope seems forlorn, and troubles abound,
When Satan roars loud, and seeks to devour,
Then Jesus sends help in the darkest of hours.

The children of God are never alone,
The Father, and Jesus, supreme on the throne,
Are closer than breathing, though hidden from sight,
So, Christian believer, go dwell in His light!

To God be the glory, great things He has done!
For wonders unbounded are sent by the Son:
Freely He gives of His bountiful grace,
His smile is our comfort, the smile of His face!

"On my bed I remember you; I think of you through the watches of the night. Because you are my help, I sing in the shadow of your wings!" Psalm 63:6,7

christian verse
for meditation

Bible references:
Psalm 63
Psalm 91
Romans 8:28-39

AN EVENING PRAYER

In God, the Lord, put I my trust,
In Him I sleep secure,
His angels watch around my bed,
Their guard is ever sure.

No foe can harm, no darkness reach
My soul at rest in Him;
His presence is my confidence,
For faith gives peace within.

Fear is the great enemy of faith. The fearful disciples of Jesus, in the midst of the storm that threatened to engulf the boat they were in, were rebuked by Jesus when he said to them, Where is your faith? We are all beset with fears at different times. Fear of sickness, fear of loneliness, fear of poverty and the greatest fear of all - the fear of death. Faith in Jesus is the great antidote to our fears, however caused. These verses were written to encourage faith in the One who is the Friend and Saviour of all who commit their lives to Him.

christian verse
for meditation

Bible references:
Isaiah 40:20-31
Luke 8:22-25
John 17

MY NEEDLESS FEAR

Though long the night and sleep escapes
And heart is full of fear,
To Jesus will I turn my eyes
My Friend who's always near.

Around me He will put His arms
And hush my soul to sleep;
Send angels to my bedside, close,
Their watch to ever keep.

Embraced in love, whilst angels watch,
Why should I needless fear?
My Saviour has all power on earth
To save His children dear!

His promise is for ever true,
No child of His He'll lose
But safely to His Father's home
Bring all those He did choose.

Why then, my soul, are you cast down
And tremble in the night?
Look up! for Jesus reigns on high
His throne is bathed in light!

And from that throne He sends His word
To children in distress,
To comfort and to cherish them,
And with His peace to bless.

Both Old and New Testaments speak of the ministry of angels. They are the messengers, or agents, of Almighty God. These unseen hosts of heavenly beings wait upon God to do His bidding. Two scriptures give us some idea of their ministry to the human race.

Matthew 18.10, "Take heed that you despise not one of these little ones; for I say unto you, That in heaven their angels do always behold the face of my Father which is in heaven."
Hebrews 1.14, "Are they not all ministering spirits, sent forth to minister for them who shall be the heirs of salvation?"

christian verse
for meditation

MINISTERING ANGELS

Around the throne of God on high,
A myriad host of angels stand;
They wait before Him, quick to fly,
Obedient to what He does command.

There they behold our Father's face,
Arrayed in aweful, holy, light,
Ready to aid us in our race,
And strengthen us with heavenly might.

These unseen hosts surround the saints,
As guardians of each child of God,
And when the human spirit faints
They quickly fly to give us aid.

In Gethsemane's darkest hour,
They watched in awe our Saviour there,
And as His soul He did outpour,
They swiftly flew His pain to share.

And in the tomb where Jesus lay,
These guardian angels vigil kept;
Told the sorrowing, at break of day,
Jesus lives! The grave He's left!

And now in heaven they serve their Lord,
These glorious spirits in radiance clothed,
Obedient to His every word
To serve His Bride, to Him betrothed.

That Bride is all the church of God,
Now brought to Jesus through His blood,
Arrayed in glory, crowned with grace,
In heaven, for us, prepares a place!

The true source of a Christian's rejoicing is not in circumstances nor in possessions, but in what God has done to give us eternal blessings which will outlast anything in this world. God so loved us that He sent His one and only Son into this world to die for us and to give us eternal life! Our rejoicing is in Jesus Christ who died and rose again and is alive for evermore! This is surely something to sing about! Whatever our outward circumstances, by faith we are enabled to look beyond these to eternal realities which transcend anything this world can offer us. The apostle Peter tells us something of this in the following verse from one of his letters.

"Though you have not seen Him, you love Him; and even though you do not see Him now, you believe in Him, and are filled with an inexpressible and glorious joy, for you are receiving the goal of your faith, the salvation of your souls." 1 Peter 1:8,9

christian verse
for meditation

Bible references:
Matthew 5:1-12
1 Peter 1:1-12

REJOICING IN GOD

Rejoice and be glad, you people of God!
For Jesus is Lord and reigns high above,
And here upon earth, the church, His true bride,
In union sweet is embraced at His side.

Drink freely, you saints, at this fountain of love,
Which flows evermore from the Father above;
This infinite fountain, eternally full,
Flowing so freely from God to us all!

Such joys beyond telling, this world cannot know,
They are kept for His loved ones, redeemed here below!
His promise is sure, His delight is to bless,
And fill with His Spirit, our souls to caress!

A foretaste of heaven, to kindle desire,
And draw us from earth to take us up higher,
And there with the angels, beholding His face,
In rapture to worship, adoring His grace!

When he was here on earth, Jesus warned his people that one of the signs of the end of the times, prior to his return to the earth, would be wars and rumours of wars. He said that nation would rise against nation and kingdom against kingdom. Also, that there would be famines and earthquakes in various places. As we hear of these things we are reminded that time is running out for the world and that Jesus will soon come back. The Christian believer should not, therefore, be dismayed by these events but look up and anticipate the Lord's return when he will judge the world and usher in a new heavens and a new earth wherein dwells righteousness.

"You will hear of wars and rumours of wars, but see to it that you are not alarmed. Such things must happen, but the end is still to come....Thus the gospel of the kingdom will be preached in the whole world, as a testimony to all nations, and then the end will come." Matthew 24:6,14

christian verse
for meditation

Bible references:
Isaiah chapter 2
Zechariah 9: 9-17
Matthew chapter 24

THE KING OF ALL THE EARTH

Jesus is King of all the earth!
He rules supreme on high;
Exalted now, from lowly birth,
Praise Him! the angels cry!

All nations must before Him bow,
This King of all the earth;
Both high and low, exalt Him now,
And own His royal worth.

You saints, this King is Saviour too,
He comes to set men free;
Abundant life He gives to you,
And perfect liberty!

He watches from that heavenly throne,
The nations bent on war,
When all the earth is made to groan,
And peace is found no more.

Why does He, then, so silent stay,
Whilst wicked men agree
To rush upon their evil way,
And spread such anarchy?

He waits, whilst nations fill their cup
Of bitterness and woe,
Then at the appointed hour rise up
And quickly overthrow!

Fear not, you saints, the time is now
To pray and intercede,
For in God's time (we know not how)
He'll judge their wicked deeds.

Rejoice, you saints, your Lord is King!
Why should you have such fear?
Lift up your hearts, rejoice and sing,
Your prayers the King does hear!

The Bible has many references to God being a hiding place for His people in time of trouble. David, the psalmist, speaks of this in the verse quoted below. We cannot be safer than when we are protected by God Himself! If the omnipotent God is our refuge when Satan assaults us, then we have nothing to fear. Jesus said, None shall pluck them out of my hand!

"The Lord is my rock and my fortress, and my deliverer: my God, my strength, in whom I will trust; my buckler, and the horn of my salvation and my high tower". Psalm 18:1

christian verse
for meditation

Bible references:
Psalm 18:1-19
Psalm 27

A ROCK AND A STRONG TOWER

In my trouble I sought your face,
And called on You, O Lord my God:
Deliver my soul, come and make haste,
And save me with your outstretched rod.

You are my Rock, my hiding place,
A tower so strong, I shall be safe
From all my foes, who now make haste
To make me fall and bring disgrace.

I shall be safe with You my God,
My shelter from the stormy blast;
My helper and my strength You are,
My safety and my hiding place!

Your care for me I will declare,
A Father's love with others share:
Lord, make them hear, though they be deaf,
And send the Spirit's quickening breath!

The Father gave us to His Son,
Whose work upon the cross was done,
To save us from eternal loss,
And keep us from a dreadful wrath.

In Him alone we are secure,
His promise is so very sure,
No one shall pluck them from my Hand,
And in My presence they shall stand!

JESUS OUR SAVIOUR

This section focuses on the Lord Jesus Christ, the only Son of God.

Jesus is the Saviour who came into this world in order to bear the sins of His people. He is God who became man in order to be the sacrifice for our sin. We celebrate His birth at Christmas; but His birth must always be linked to His death. He was born to die in order to be the Saviour of men.

Jesus did not begin His existence when He came into the world. He is eternal and came from heaven that first Christmas day. We began to be when we were born. Jesus "came" here and took our human nature to Himself so that He could suffer and die in our place.

As a true man He was tempted and suffered trials just like us. The Bible tells us that He was touched with the feeling of our infirmities. He knows how we feel because He has been here, and lived here. And yet He was without sin. That was essential for He could not have paid the price for our sin if He had sin of His own to die for.

God has set Jesus forth as the only Saviour of men. No man comes to the Father except through Jesus Christ. There is no other name given amongst men whereby we can be saved.

It is only through the shedding of His blood that our sins can be covered. His blood cleanses from all sin. His blood overcomes Satan, that great enemy of our souls, and silences his accusations of guilt against us.

The name of Jesus is the most precious name in all the world to believers. It is the name whereby we prevail in prayer. It is the name by which we come to God. It is the name that all the angels in heaven worship, day and night.

May these verses enable you to see how wonderful this Person is and just what He has done for us so that you, too, may worship Him.

We say, What's in a name? The name of Jesus tells us what he is like and what he has done. The name means Saviour. When he was born God commanded that he should be called Jesus for he would save his people from their sins.

Christians, in all ages, testify to the power of using that name. When troubled they have called out his name and have been comforted and delivered from their fears. Our prayers are only heard by God when offered in that name. God is pleased when we call upon Jesus' name whatever our need might be.

"And the angel said unto her, Fear not, Mary: for you have found favour with God. And, behold, you shall conceive in your womb, and bring forth a son, and shall call his name JESUS". Luke 1:30,31

Bible references:
Luke 1:26-38
Luke 2:1-20
Titus 2:11-14
Revelation 22:7-17

THE NAME OF JESUS

What sweetness rests in Jesus' Name,
The Name we hold so dear;
The Name that soothes and heals our wounds,
And drives away all fear.

His Name adored by angel hosts,
Who stand around His throne,
And loved by men of broken hearts,
Who trust in Him alone.

What joy He brings to hearts made soft,
From sin and shame made free;
To hearts remade to be like His,
His blood our only plea.

Our Jesus stands astride this world,
His arms outstretched in love;
He calls, but O, so few do hear,
And heed the heavenly Dove.

O taste and see, what pleasure's found
In feasting on His love;
Like honey from the honeycomb
That comes from heaven above.

When we look back on life we may well feel that our lives have been unfruitful and wasted. But God does not judge as men judge. He looks on the heart not on what we may, or may not, have done. The fruitfulness that God looks for is a changed life that reflects the life of Jesus. A life changed through the new birth whereby the Holy Spirit comes to dwell within us.

Our love for Jesus is what interests our heavenly Father. We may not have achieved much in life, and we may consider ourselves failures, but God may see something that no one else can see, something that delights Him because it is a reflection of His Son in us.

Jesus said, "I am the True Vine, you are the branches: he that abides in me, and I in him, the same brings forth much fruit: for without me you can do nothing." John 15:5

christian verse
for meditation

Bible references:
Luke 1:26-38
Luke 2:1-20
Titus 2:11-14
Revelation 22:7-17

THE TRUE VINE

Upon this earth the Father planned
To plant a Vine with His own hand:
This Vine would grow, much fruit to bear,
The life of God, for man to share.

This Vine is Jesus, God's dear Son,
Who came to earth our race to run,
To save mankind from Satan's hand
And guide us to the Promised Land.

Born of Mary, our nature wears,
God as man, to man appears,
The son of man, yet Son of God,
Bears our sin and sheds His blood.

This Vine, much fruit it was to bear,
The gospel calls all men to hear,
Believe and live! to Jesus come!
His life to share, His victory won.

The men of faith, it's branches are,
He is the Root, His life we share,
And from that Root to us will flow
The life of God, and fruit to show.

Joined to Him by faith alone,
Who died for us, and did atone
For all our sins at Calvary,
And dying there He set men free.

In Jesus, then, much fruit we bear,
With lives now full of holy cheer;
Without Him there is nought we do
That pleases God, nor fruit to show.

Abide in Him the one true Vine,
For there in Christ your fruits will shine:
And so the Father glorified,
Your life will bless as you abide.

Someone who is told that they have a terminal illness is brought face to face with the things that really matter in life. Gabrielle, a young woman with terminal cancer, was one such person. These verses were written for her and for all those who find themselves cast upon God, for whatever reason. This poem is a poem of hope for our God is a God of hope! It reminds us that our only hope for time and for eternity rests in a Person who died and rose again, even Jesus Christ, whom to know is eternal life.

"For everything that was written in the past was written to teach us, so that through endurance and the encouragement of the scriptures we might have hope." Romans 15:4

christian verse
for meditation

JESUS, OUR ONLY HOPE

When Jesus walked upon this earth
The people thronged to hear His word.
Such words they never heard before
From Him whom angels all adore.

Who is this Man, who understands
The pains and needs on every hand?
Who stoops to sinners in their plight,
Who came to earth to give us light.

Who is this Man, with eyes so kind,
Who came from heaven, lost souls to find?
Who had no home nor place to sleep,
Yet broken hearts He made to leap!

This Man, He walked upon the sea,
And stilled the storm so quietly:
His friends, in awe, did there behold,
And wonder at this Man so bold.

He healed the sick and raised the dead,
A crippled man rolled up his bed!
They leaped and danced, who had been lame,
And spread abroad His marvellous Name!

He gave His life that we might live:
He rose, eternal life to give,
To bring to heaven a host of men,
Saved through His bloodmade whole again!

Abundant life, He came to give
To weary souls, that they might live!
No more to walk in sad despair
But live His life, His joy to share!

This Man is Jesus, God's own Son,
Whose love unnumbered souls has won,
He beckons, calls you by your name,
Now bids you sing in heaven's refrain!

Reach out in faith, believe in Him,
And healing virtue will flow in:
With sins forgiven, a home above,
Your soul will rest in Jesus love!

Separation from friends and those we love is always sad and difficult. But for the Christian believer there is a bond with fellow-believers that neither time nor distance can break. We are all joined to one another in Jesus Christ. And we all meet together in the same place each day. Where is that place? It is what the Old Testament calls the Mercy Seat, which is the place of prayer where God meets with us. There, we bear one another up before God and realise that the same Holy Spirit indwells us all.

"Now you are the body of Christ, and each one of you is a part of it".
I Corinthians 12:27

ALL ONE IN CHRIST

Where'er we are on earth below,
There is a place to which we go,
Where kindred spirits love to meet:
It is at Christ's own Mercy Seat.

There, in Christ, we all are one,
Beloved of Him whose love has won
Our hearts, which now to Him belong,
And there we praise Him in our song.

To Him we bring our hearts desires,
And there He sends the Spirit's fire,
Anoints us to proclaim His name,
And sends us out with hearts aflame.

So, when we part, we're ever bound
By cords of love which Christ has wound
Around our hearts, which then He keeps,
To draw us to the Mercy Seat.

Let us keep faith with Christ our King,
And to His feet petitions bring,
And bear each other to the Throne
For in His name we now are one.

So when we part we still may bring
Petitions to our heavenly King,
And hold each other's hands on high
To Jesus, who is ever nigh.

When He was here on earth, Jesus delighted to call himself Son of man. He readily identified himself with us because it was for us that He came into this world. It was as a true man that He suffered and died for our sins. His humanity is as real as ours, even though He was true God. He knew what it was to be hungry and tired. He wept at the grave of Lazarus. He knew pain and anguish of heart. He knew suffering like no man has ever known. And yet He is the Lord.

"Let all the house of Israel know assuredly that God has made this Jesus, whom you crucified, both Lord and Christ." Acts 2:36

"You call me Master and Lord: and you say well; for so I am". John 13:13

"For it is written, As I live, says the Lord, every knee shall bow to me, and every tongue confess to God". Romans 14:11

christian verse
for meditation

Bible references:
Psalm 2
Matthew 14:13-36
Acts 2:22-36

JESUS IS LORD

Jesus, you are Lord of all,
Heaven's great King to earth come down,
Sinners for to find and call
To the glory and a crown!

Here on earth you walked with men,
Sought the lost and healed the sick,
Raised the dead, gave life again,
New hope to all mankind did bring.

You stilled the wind and calmed the waves
Upon the lake engulfed with storm:
For nature knows the One who speaks,
He who is God in human form!

And demons, too, they know that voice,
And tremble at His stern command
To loose the prisoners they have bound,
And bring to nought what Satan planned.

He came to save the sons of men
Who, in their blindness, know not Him,
From every race, from all mankind
Their place to take, die for their sin.

So let us praise such matchless grace,
That brought the Saviour down from heaven,
Whose love for all the human race
Excels all thought and all our ken!

Because God has done the greatest thing possible, so He will do all the other, lesser, things. So free is the grace of God that all we have to do is to receive!

This God with whom we deal has never had to receive anything from anybody. There is no one to whom God has ever been in debt. A long time ago God said, If I had need of anything, would I tell you? If the living God had need of anything He would cease to be God. But we have need of God. We are totally dependent upon Him for everything, starting with our existence and our very breath, for time and all eternity.

And here is the wonder; God has no need of us yet He seeks us. We have need of Him but do not seek Him!

"He that spared not His own Son, but delivered him up for us all, how shall He not with him also freely give us all things." Romans 8.32

christian verse
for meditation

Bible references:
Isaiah chapter 53
Matthew 27:26-54

THE SACRIFICE OF CALVARY

In God's all-wise, eternal, love
He freely gave His only Son;
In love he was delivered up,
His precious and beloved One.

He spared him not, our souls to win,
But sent him from th'eternal throne;
For only he could save from sin,
Lost souls to win and bring them home.

What price was this, that God did pay,
The sacrifice of Calvary?
His only Son, who died that day,
Paid with his blood to set us free.

There was no price that we could pay,
(Our debts had mounted to the sky),
But Jesus left his home that day
And sped to earth for us to die.

Upon the cross he bled and died,
For blood alone must cleanse from sin;
In anguish and in sorrow cried
Father, forgive, and take them in.

A holy God, beheld His Son,
And saw the sacrifice complete,
Our sin removed, and heaven now won,
With Satan crushed beneath his feet.

How, then, shall God not freely give
All lesser things His people need?
The One who died is he who lives
To bless his saints and intercede.

Then let us all our pleas prepare,
And boldly come to him who died,
Assured that he will hear our prayer
And send the answer from the skies!

When we speak of the beauty of Jesus we speak not so much of physical as moral and spiritual beauty. Here upon earth He suffered for us and carried the great burden of our sin. That is what Isaiah refers to when, below, he says of Him, that, "He has no form nor comeliness that we should desire Him". And yet, Jesus has a beauty that draws men and women to Him. It is a beauty that we do not have and yet for which our hearts yearn. It is the beauty of holiness. And the Bible tells us the day is coming that when we see Him we shall be like Him! His moral beauty will be reproduced in all who have put their trust in Him. However much sin may have spoiled us in this life, all will be restored to the perfection of Christ's beauty in the next. This is the prospect that God sets before all His people!

"Your eyes will see the King in His beauty; they will see the land that is very far off." Isaiah 33:17

"He has no form or comeliness; and when we see him there is no beauty that we should desire Him. He is despised and rejected of men a man of sorrows and acquainted with grief, and we hid, as it were, our faces from Him. Surely He has borne our griefs and carried our sorrows!" Isaiah 53:2-4

"We have seen his glory, the glory of the One and Only, who came from the Father, full of grace and truth." John 1:14

christian verse
for meditation

THE BEAUTY OF JESUS

Dear Jesus, come and fill this place,
And let us see your lovely face,
And then with you for evermore,
To love and praise and to adore!

We want none else, yourself alone:
Come, make our hearts a royal throne,
So make them soft and joyful too,
A heaven on earth, a feast with you.

Shew us your face and let us see
The beauty angels share with thee,
Nought else but this can satisfy,
O let us see you e'er we die.

No joys on earth with you compare,
Like morn they fade in sun's bright glare,
Your joys unspeakable, and holy too,
Reserved for all in love with you.

What grace, what love, from heaven's great King,
That with the angels we can sing
Glory to God; our hearts o'erflow
As here we sing on earth below.

Jesus is King, let earth adore,
Trees, clap your hands, let oceans roar,
Angels and men, your voices raise
And sing your great Redeemer's praise!

The name of Jesus has been the most revered and precious name throughout the Christian era. One great hymn writer of past ages wrote a lovely hymn that encapsulates everything lovely about that name,- "How sweet the name of Jesus sounds, In a believer's ear, It soothes his sorrows, heals his wounds, And drives away his fear!" It is a name full of meaning and hope. It means "Saviour" and it has been the name that countless Christians have always called upon when in need. And it is the name that, when used by believers in prayer, has power with God. It invests the Christian with an authority without which his prayers would not be heard by God. It was because he loved us that he came to earth as Jesus.

"If you shall ask anything in My Name, I will do it." John 14.14

christian verse
for meditation

Bible references:
Isaiah chapter 53
John 13:1-17

THE LOVE OF JESUS

Jesus, your love has won my soul,
Your presence within has made me whole,
How sweet your Name for me to hear,
And tell it forth both far and near!

This Name, it tells us who you are,
The Saviour sent by God from afar
To bear our sins, make them His own,
And shed His blood, for us to atone.

For our iniquities was He bruised
And our transgressions, wounded too;
Marred was His face, more than any man,
As in our place fulfilled God's plan.

Jesus our Surety, took our place,
A substitute, ('twas all of grace),
That God should send His own dear Son,
Our souls to save from wrath to come.

Jesus, your love has won my heart
That you should let me have a part,
And share with you such joy and peace,
With pleasures that can never cease.

Let God be praised by all on earth,
Tell forth our Jesus, tell out His worth,
Declare His Name to all mankind
That all who seek shall surely find.

God with us! What assurance these words give us! But can we take them to ourselves? Yes, all the promises of God are "Yes" and "Amen" in Jesus Christ. He is both God and man - Immanuel. No man can look on God and live, the Bible tells us. Yet in Jesus we see God and are safe. Jesus himself said - He that has seen me has seen the Father. Immanuel - God with you and I, never to leave us or forsake us!

"The virgin will be with child and will give birth to a son, and they will call his name Immanuel , which means "God with us". Matthew 1.23

Bible references:
Matthew 1:18-25

IMMANUEL

What thoughts arise from that dear Name,
Immanuel, God with us!
It tells us that the Saviour came,
The love of God to show us.

It tells us of the God who loves
The men He has created;
That from the throne in heaven above
Has sent His Son, long promised.

Incarnate God, in manger lies,
With cattle lowing round Him,
And angels from the starry skies,
With joy, on Him attending.

The shepherds with their flocks that night,
With glory shining round them,
Are filled with wonder at the sight
Of angel hosts descending.

God thus appears in human form,
A babe in arms now lying,
Immanuel, a Saviour born,
That wondrous Christmas morning!

We are told in Matthew's gospel that Jesus received that name because of what it meant, Saviour. The verse quoted below tells us that He came to save us from our sins. The Old Testament name of Joshua is the Hebrew equivalent of Jesus, and means the same. Many people accept that Jesus was a good man and that he was a prophet. Whilst that is true it does not go far enough for Jesus is the eternal Son of God. He entered this world by becoming a man in order to suffer and to die for the sins of men. And though He became man He did not cease to be God! He is both God and man! In this amazing union He has joined the Godhead to our humanity. He has thus bridged and unbridgeable gap, joining the uncreated God to created humanity in such a union that it makes it possible for sinful men and women to know the Unknowable. Thus He said, he that has seen me has seen the Father.

"And she (Mary) shall bring forth a son, and thou shalt call his name JESUS; for he shall save his people from their sins". Matthew 1:21

Bible references:
Mark chapter 15
Luke chapter 23

THE MAN CHRIST JESUS

On Sion's hill stands Sion's King
The mighty God, Lord of ev'rything!
Salvation from His God did bring,
This man, whose name is Jesus!

His eyes behold the worlds afar,
His hands uphold the furthest star,
Those hands have nail prints, His side a scar,
This man, whose name is Jesus!

He came from heaven to live with men,
Love incarnate did descend,
This mighty God to us did bend,
This man, whose name is Jesus!

He was a boy, learned Joseph's trade,
Yet all things from eternity made!
In Nazareth's school, there learned and played,
This man, whose name is Jesus!

He grew as man, fulfilled God's plan,
This Son of God and son of man,
Right to the end our race he ran,
This man, whose name is Jesus!

He went about and healed the sick,
Gave blind men sight and made rejoice!
He stilled the storms, they knew his voice!
This man, whose name is Jesus!

He cured the lame and raised the dead,
At Lazarus' grave his tears were shed,
His heart so moved by sin's dark tread!
This man, whose name is Jesus!

Satan's work, to destroy he came,
Enter'd the fight in his Father's name,
Released the captives to sin and shame,
This man, whose name is Jesus!

To the cross he went, sin's price to pay,
The maddened crowd shouting crucify!
But, friend, it was for you and I!
This man, whose name is Jesus!

Between two thieves he bled and died,
Mocked, scourged, he was there crucified,
A spear thrust into his side,
This man, whose name is Jesus!

But death, it's hold, it could not last,
He broke those bands that hold men fast!
He rose triumphant, death now past!
This man, whose name is Jesus!

And now, dear friend, what do you say
Of this great King who died that day?
His name you know, so now embrace
This Mighty God, this King of grace!

Christmas welcomes the birth of Jesus Christ. This amazing fact is all too often lost on a materialistic world, that the eternal Son of God should leave the bliss of heaven in order to become a man so that He could share our lives and, through the cross, enable us to share His. The great question we should ask ourselves is, Has Christmas happened to us? Has Jesus been born in us? This is what Jesus himself called the new birth, born again of the Spirit of God whereby we are made new men and women by regeneration of the Spirit. Christmas as a historical fact is wonderful and we should enter fully into great rejoicing for this, and not just at Christmas! But even more wonderful is when it happens to us personally! Has it happened to you?

"And the shepherds came with haste and found Mary and Joseph, and the Babe lying in a manger." Luke 2:16

CHRISTMAS

From heaven there came the angels' song,
Of Jesus Christ, who, promised long,
Descends to men of humble heart
To save from sin, new life impart!

He came to save a lost mankind,
The Shepherd for His sheep to find,
From heaven's heights to earth below
The Saviour stooped so very low.

From heaven's throne to stable bare,
He swiftly flew, our life to share;
'Midst cattle in the dark of night
Was born the Christ, the promised Light!

Upon the hills the shepherds gazed,
As hosts of angels sang His praise
And welcomed Him whom Mary bore,
The Babe whom heaven and earth adores.

To see that sight the shepherds ran
Down to the place at Bethlehem!
And marvelling, at His feet they fell,
In wonder lost, a world to tell.

And wise men from the east then came
To find this King of royal fame,
With priceless gifts they worshipped there
The Babe in stable rude and bare.

How few there were that Christmas day
Who found the Christ just where He lay;
And so today they pass Him by,
This Jesus, who was born to die.

Die for the sins of all mankind,
To save our souls (He is so kind),
So see Him now, this Christmas day
The One who takes all sin away!

The Christian gospel centres on the cross on which our Lord and
Saviour, Jesus Christ, died for the sins of all men. His was an atoning
death in that it fully met the just demands of a holy God for a broken
law on the part of all mankind. No other sacrifice was sufficient to
pay the price for man's sin. The well-known hymn "There was a
green hill far away", puts it perfectly in the verse:

"There was no other good enough
To pay the price of sin;
He only could unlock the gate
Of heaven and let us in!"

An essential part of Jesus' sacrifice were the events that took place
in the Garden of Gethsemane on the night of His betrayal by
Judas Iscariot. This is where the battle with the powers of darkness
was fought by the Lord Jesus, and won, prior to the cross. His prayers
and agony in the garden are deeply moving and profound. And we
need to remind ourselves that He did this as a mortal man, in the
strength of a man, like you and I. Remember, too, as you read
this, that He did it for you and me because He loved us! If we are
ever tempted to doubt that God loves us we should go back
to Gethsemane and watch the Son of God as He wrestled with
the powers of darkness to deliver us from them.

"Then came they, and laid hands on Jesus, and took Him."
Matthew 26:50

christian verse
for meditation

Bible references:
Isaiah chapter 53
Matthew 26:36-46

GETHSEMANE

Gethsemane, Gethsemane,
The place where Jesus trod,
On that dark night, to pray He came,
The blessed Son of God.

With Peter, John and James, He came,
To comfort in distress
To wait and watch and pray, He said,
Whilst praying, sorely pressed.

It was a night of darkness deep,
Abroad were powers of hell,
That sought the Saviour now to keep
From this, His Father's will.

It was the time when Satan's head
Would soon be sorely bruised,
His Father, long ago, had said
This work His Son would choose.

The thickened darkness soon engulfed
This blessed Son of God,
And sore amazed and sorrowful,
He kneeled upon the sod.

Upon His face in agony,
He cried unto His God
"O, if it is just possible
Do please this cup withhold"!

No answer came on that dark night,
But still He cried to God;
Whilst others slept within His sight
He there sweat drops of blood!

A second time He went to pray
In greater agony!
"If this cup pass not away,
Thy will, it pleases Me"!

But still disciples slept that night,
And still the Saviour prayed,
Against the powers of hell did fight,
Until He was betrayed!

Into the garden Judas came,
With soldiers rough and rude,
To take our Jesus by deceit
With a great multitude.

To Caiaphas they took Him first,
Who roughly sought to know,
"Art thou the Son of God, the Christ?
Now tell us, is it true?"

"Thou hast said", was His reply,
"Hereafter you shall see,
The Son of Man in power on high,
Enthroned, eternally".

Enraged, these men did spit at Him,
And smote that lovely face;
With hands so coarse and cruelly
Did vent their spite and hate.

The powers of hell would do their worst
And use the hands of men,
With violence and evil thirst
Destroy this blessed One!

Continued

christian verse
for meditation

Bible references:
Isaiah chapter 53
Matthew 26:36-46

GETHSEMANE

CONTINUED

But from His task He would not flinch,
He faced the deadly foe;
This Son of Man gave not an inch,
As fell the fatal blow!

A blow that was men's just desert,
The Saviour took Himself!
The wrath of God about Him girt,
To give us life and health!

If to Gethsemane you go,
By faith, to see this grief,
Consider how those tears did flow
To bring you such relief!

Come to Him now, open your heart,
Receive this Saviour true,
And know that you can have a part
In all He did for you!

The coming of Jesus Christ into the world was the greatest event in history. It was an event that spanned the unbridgeable gap between that which is God and that which is not God. In other words the immortal put on mortality in order to die for the sins of men. But, also, it will forever remain the greatest event in history because it was the most stupendous demonstration of the love of God towards all humanity.

How do you measure love? The apostle, John, said, "In this is love, not that we loved God, but that He loved us and sent His Son to be the propitiation for our sins."
1 John 4:10

And Jesus said, "Greater love has no one than this, than to lay down his life for his friends. You are my friends if you do whatsoever I command you."
John 15:13,14

Love is measured, not so much by words, but by actions. The supreme demonstration of God's love for men and women is in that great fact of Jesus dying in our place and taking our sins upon himself so that we might be forgiven and find a place in heaven when we die.

"For God so loved the world that He gave His one and only Son that whosoever believes in him should not perish but have everlasting life."
John 3:16

christian verse
for meditation

LOVE CAME DOWN

In love, the Saviour came from heaven,
To seek and save the lost;
Unmeasured depths He plumbed for us,
But love, it spurned the cost.

On wings of mercies, fast He flew,
Watched by angelic hosts,
In wonder, gazed at His descent,
To live with men below.

What love is this that brought Him down
From realms of highest bliss?
To lay aside His glorious crown,
Redeem that which was His!

No man can plumb that heart of love
Which beats within His breast;
God only knows the love of God
Which seeks, that it may bless.

He came to save, not to condemn,
To set the captives free,
That all who come to Him by faith
May live, and so might see.

Yes, see the love of God in Christ
Made plain in human form,
The One who walked upon the sea
And stilled the raging storm.

And so He'll still the storms of life
That trouble hearts of men,
Give peace that takes away all strife,
Lost years, restore again.

The inspired writers of the scriptures were at a loss to find words that would adequately express the beauty of Jesus Christ. In His condescension, the Spirit of God used homely expressions that everyone could understand, and so in the Old Testament book, the Song of Solomon, Jesus is described in terms of flowers. Flowers that are beautiful to look at and having an enchanting perfume. Listen as the Spirit describes the beauty of Jesus in poetic language –

"I am the Rose of Sharon, and the lily of the valleys. Like a lily among thorns so is my love among the daughters. Like an apple tree among the trees of the woods, so is my beloved among the sons. I sat down under his shade with great delight, and his fruit was sweet to my taste." Song of Solomon 2:1-3

Unlike flowers, the beauty of Jesus never fades. And His beauty is that inner beauty which radiates from Him. A moral and spiritual beauty which is that which pleases God and which will one day be ours. The Bible tells us that –"We know that when He is revealed, we shall be like Him, for we shall see Him as He is." 1 John 3:2

Jesus is the perfection of beauty; a radiance that is awesome and before which we must bow in adoration and worship.

christian verse
for meditation

Bible references:
Song of Solomon 2:1-3
Ezekiel 47:1-12
John 7:37-39

THE FAIREST FLOWER

Of all the flowers that God has made,
The fairest are in heaven:
And there, the fairest of them all
Is Jesus, Rose of Sharon!

Amongst ten thousand stands He alone,
None with Him can compare:
His beauty draws the souls of men,
With them His beauty shares.

His presence lights the heavenly courts,
And hearts of men on earth:
He fills the longing soul with joy,
Perfumes our paths with mirth.

Unlike the flowers on earth that fade,
This Flower of Heaven, never!
For endless waters from God's throne
Flow boundless, freely, ever!

These waters are the life of God,
And flow to earth from heaven:
This Jesus is that spring of life
To sinners, freely given.

So let us gladly praise our God
Who plants His flowers on earth,
Where Jesus walks, unseen by men,
This Man of royal birth.

This parable that Jesus gave is meant to tell us, not only that we are all like the prodigal in that we are away from our heavenly Father's house, and need to return, but also it tells us something of the love of the father. Someone has said that another title of the parable could be "The Waiting Father". That is true, for if one observes the father in the story we see a depth of love for his wayward son that daily looks and waits for his return and when he sees him coming he runs to meet him and embraces him.

This is meant to tell us of how much our Heavenly Father loves us and yearns for us to come home to be blessed. Notice, too, that there is no condemnation of the son by the father, but rather he throws him a party! When we come to Jesus and repent of sin he does not condemn us but forgives us and embraces us in His love and makes us welcome.

"Jesus said unto him (Thomas), I am the Way, the Truth and the Life: no man cometh unto the Father but by me." John 14:6

"And when he was a great way off, his father saw him, and had compassion on him, and ran, and fell on his neck and kissed him." Luke 15:20

"There is therefore now no condemnation to them which are in Christ Jesus." Romans 8:1

christian verse
for meditation

THE DOOR TO HEAVEN

I am the Way, the Truth, the Life,
The Door by which men come;
By Me they enter into heaven
And find a welcome home.

That home is where the Father lives,
A place of light and joy,
For there the Father gladly gives
All pleasures to enjoy.

There, too, a Father's kind embrace
Awaits us at the door;
There are no words this can express
But simply to adore.

Look up, dear saint, your home awaits,
A mansion in the sky;
A place that Jesus has prepared
To live with Him on high!

Jesus is the God-man. He is both God and man through the mystery of the incarnation. It was divine love that brought him into this world so that he might redeem for himself, from amongst sinful men and women, a church that would be his bride in heaven.

Because it was man who sinned it needed to be a man who had to pay the price of sin in order to be the Redeemer. But what man was there in the whole world who was without any sin of his own for it must be a sinless man to be the Redeemer? Mrs Alexander in her hymn – "There is a green hill far away" – put it perfectly when she wrote –

"There was no other good enough,
To pay the price of sin,
He only could unlock the gate
Of heaven, and let us in."

Who is this man? the poem asks. It is Jesus Christ, the man of Galilee, who came here to be our Saviour. Do you know him?

"For God hath made him to be a sin offering for us, who knew no sin."
2Corinthians 5:21

christian verse
for meditation

Bible references:
Matthew 1:18-25
Luke 23:18-47
Revelation 21:2-7

WHO IS THIS MAN?

Who is this Man with eyes of love,
Who left the heights of heaven above?
To dwell with men on earth below,
His love and grace on us bestow!

Who is this Man, with eyes of fire,
Who walked this earth with such desire?
To seek and save souls that are lost
And give His life, whate'er the cost.

Who is this Man who wept to see
The curse of sin, man's enemy?
Yet loved poor sinners in their need
And came, the promised holy Seed.

Who is this Man with arms outstretched
Upon the cross by sinners fixed?
Whose angels watched with wondering gaze
The Father's Son, His gift of grace.

Who is this Man, who left the grave,
And rose victorious, souls to save?
Returned back to His Father's side
And waits with joy to greet His bride!

The Man is Jesus, God's own Son,
Who countless souls His love has won!
Now own Him King, His right to reign,
And for His saints a heaven to gain!

THE HEART'S CRY

christian verse
for meditation

Sections One to Four of this series have dealt with the great themes of Creation, the all-embracing love and kindness of Almighty God and the pre-eminence of Jesus Christ, God's Son, who came into this world to be the Saviour of sinful men and women.

Section Five addresses the greatest of all issues known to man, and that is our need of inner peace; the cry of the heart for meaning and purpose in life. Despite prosperity and an abundance of ways in which to enjoy life, never has there been a time when the emptiness of lives has been more apparent.

Christians, down through the years, have all proved that the only remedy for an aching heart is to know Jesus Christ. He is the great lover of men's souls and within each one of us is a place which only He can occupy and thus bring God's peace.

This peace is described in the Bible as the peace of God which passes all understanding.

These poems all address this great need in the hearts of people of all backgrounds and cultures. May they direct each reader to the only One who can meet the deepest needs of every heart, even Jesus the Saviour.

When God calls us we must listen. Have you heard His voice? Not an audible voice but that inward, insistent, voice from which we cannot escape. God never gives up on us unless we deliberately reject Him. He pursues us through all the twists and turns of life until He finds us. Wherever we run or hide, God is there, calling us to Himself because He loves us and wants us. Stop running and listen!

"Here I am! I stand at the door and knock. If anyone hears my voice and opens the door, I will come in and eat with him, and he with me." Revelation 3:20

christian verse
for meditation

THE VOICE

O Lord, Your grace has made me free,
Free from the law of sin and death;
My sin is gone and now I see;
Now see, where once I was so blind:
Now breathe the air of love divine.

Without that grace, I must remain
Fast bound in sin, alive but dead;
I cannot see, nor heaven gain,
Whate'er my works or tears are shed,
For sin, it's chains, are chains of death.

I did not know that I was dead,
This world, it's pleasures, filled my soul:
The days, they passed, new joys they fed
My hungry soul. Yet is this all?
A Voice within began to call.

From whence this Voice so kind and true,
That knew this heart that longed for peace?
The Voice within, it louder grew,
Disturbed my thoughts, yet would not cease
Nor would it let me rest at ease.

I could not rest, and though I tried
To flee this Voice of love divine,
It followed hard, I could not hide,
Where'er I went that Voice so kind,
It traced my steps and filled my mind.

The day then dawned, (I now rejoice)
When grace, my eyes had opened wide.
The Voice, it spoke of One whose choice
To bear my sin and pay the price,
Upon the cross, a sacrifice!

'Twas grace alone that made me free,
Free from the law of sin and death!
My sin now gone, my only plea
That Jesus died, His blood He shed,
And rose victorious from the dead!

These verses were written for someone who confessed that, despite their material success in life, and despite having many friends and enjoying many of the pleasures this world offers, still could not find anything to satisfy a deep, inner, hunger and emptiness. In the verse quoted below, the psalmist describes it as the soul panting after God, for God is the only true reality and alone can satisfy that deep hunger of the soul.

"As the deer pants for streams of water, so my soul pants for you O God.
My soul thirsts for God, for the living God. When can I go and meet with God? My tears have been my food day and night, while men say to me all day long, Where is your God?" Psalm 42:103

christian verse
for meditation

Bible references:
Matthew 6:19-24
Luke 12:13-34

THE EMPTY PLACE WITHIN

There is a place so deep within
No one but God can enter in:
And there my empty soul does crave
Some meaning, or Someone to save.

I've tried the joys this world holds out,
The fun, the laughter, friends without;
But none could reach that place within,
Nor can I there those pleasures bring.

I sadly thought that I was king,
My own small world to rule within,
But I have found that my great need
Is Someone who my soul will feed.

Each day I thirst, and hunger, still,
And fondly hope that soon I will
Find peace and joy to satisfy,
Or else I fear that I shall die.

They tell me that there is a God
Who made that empty place within,
That He alone can fill that space
And give me peace, all through His grace.

Where can I find this God who knows
The way I take? whose Spirit blows
Within the souls of men like me
Who crave for such reality?

My friend, this God is Jesus Christ,
Who came to earth for such as you,
Just call His Name, confess your sin,
And He will fill that space within.

This is a prayer to the Triune God. The word means "three". Almighty God is one God but three Persons, the Father, the Son and the Holy Spirit. This is a great mystery but there are many places in scripture to show that God is One whilst being three Persons within the Godhead. This prayer addresses each Person in turn.

"Jesus said, if a man loves me, he will keep my words: and my Father will love him, and we will come unto him, and make our home with him." John 14:23

Bible references:
Matthew 6:5-15
Luke 11:1-13

A PRAYER

Love me, hold me,
O God, my Father;
Tell me, show me,
The mystery of Your love.

Love me, keep me,
Jesus, my Saviour;
Cleanse me, wash me,
In your precious blood
.

Surround me, fill me,
Dear Spirit, so gentle;
Lift me, move me,
To tell of Jesus' love.

Hear me, bless me,
O God, so glorious;
Keep me for ever
In your boundless love.

Most of us carry burdens with us. It may be chronic sickness, or children who have kicked over the traces and gone astray. It may be connected with relationships at home or at work. It may be money problems. Whatever those burdens are Jesus invites us to give them to Him. He has the compassion and the strength to carry those burdens for us. He doesn't want us to be bowed down with the cares and worries of this world. He tells us not to worry about the future for worrying won't accomplish anything. Our future is in Jesus' hands, hands that have the nail marks of His suffering for us on the cross; evidence enough of His love for us! The Bible tells us that He has borne our griefs and carried our sorrows. He comes alongside us day by day and says to us, Let me carry your burden for you. I can manage what is too heavy and difficult for you to carry.

Jesus said, "Come unto me, all you who are weary and burdened, and I will give you rest. Take my yoke upon you and learn from me, for I am gentle and humble in heart, and you will find rest for your souls. For my yoke is easy and my burden is light." Matthew 11:28-30

christian verse
for meditation

LIFTED BURDENS

Bowed down and pressed by burdens sore,
When darkness did abound;
No light, no hope, it seemed to her,
Until a voice did sound.

The voice of Jesus then did speak
Into her troubled heart,
Did penetrate the darkness deep,
Made hells' dark hosts depart!

The voice, so gentle and so kind,
Revealed a Father's heart,
A Saviour's love for her so dear,
To her He did impart.

The music of that heavenly voice,
Made angels stand in awe!
Enraptured, too, this hard-pressed soul
On wings of love did soar.

To her He then revealed His face,
So tender and so kind,
And all her sadness soon gave place,
To joys e'er she could find.

From heaven alone such joys are found,
At God's right hand are they;
And pleasures, too, for evermore,
That none can take away!

Loneliness is something we all fear, especially as we get older. For many reasons more and more people are living alone, especially the elderly. With no one to talk to and share everyday things is the lot of many elderly people, some of whom are house-bound and seldom see new faces. Even younger people who, for whatever reason, have lost their partner face the prospect of returning home to an empty house and no one to talk to. Loneliness is one of the distinguishing characteristics of our age and it is a sad commentary on the church that so little is done to reach out to such people. These verses are a prayer for such people and would direct them to look to Jesus, who lived on this earth and Himself knew not only loneliness but was despised and rejected of men and finally crucified. This One is now risen and rules in heaven, waiting to come to all who would seek Him in their loneliness.

"God sets the solitary in families; He brings out those who are bound into prosperity." Psalm 68:6

Bible references:
Psalm 68:1-10

THE SOLITARY SOUL

O love of God, come fill my heart
My fear to drive away:
Your love is all I really need,
A Friend for every day.

Why must I dwell with none to share
Life's precious moments here?
To know a gentle touch or look,
Would banish petty fear.

To walk alone, is this my lot
The Lord has portioned me?
Ah, no! His jealous love is such
He wants to walk with me!

He wants me for Himself alone!
And will not share my love:
He bids me just to trust His word,
And so His friendship prove.

That lesson learned, I then will know
No fear of solitude:
In faith and love I then will grow
To share this precious food.

Here in verse is the true testimony of a young man upon being born again. Jesus said that except a man be born again he cannot see the kingdom of God. How true that is! Until the Spirit of God comes to us and opens our eyes we simply fail to see the spiritual reality of Jesus and his finished work upon the cross for us. But once our eyes are opened we see what we failed to see before. The Bible tells us that if any man be in Christ he is a new creation. This is a far-reaching and radical change which results in a transformation of the whole man. Some of the results from this are expressed in these verses.

"Therefore if anyone is in Christ, he is a new creation; old things have passed away; behold, all things have become new." 2 Corinthians 5:17

A YOUNG MAN'S TESTIMONY

My eyes were closed, I could not see,
Until, dear Lord, you came to me,
Restored my sight, called me by name,
Removed my guilt, and all my shame.

What sights, then, met my wondering gaze,
For all seemed changed; I was amazed!
Creation's form, a brighter hue?
I asked myself, Can this be true?

Ah yes, with new-born eyes beheld
Creation's beauty now revealed
In brighter colours than before;
My heart rose up, to heaven did soar!

With lighter step I now did walk,
And God's great love was all my talk.
That He should love a sinful man
And tell him of Redemption's plan!

That Jesus came to earth for me!
To take my sins and set me free!
New life to give, with joys untold,
A thousand blessings to unfold!

He said to me, you are My son;
From Satan's hand your soul I've won,
For Jesus died upon the cross,
To bear your sin at such great cost.

And now He sends His Spirit, free,
To fill my heart, and show to me
The things of Christ, and feed my soul,
So make my wounded spirit whole.

This Jesus is my all in all,
My Saviour, Lord, on whom I call,
He hears my prayer, attends my cry,
In troubles oft, draws very nigh.

He'll never leave, and not forsake
The soul who Him in faith does take;
For faith does bind Him to our heart;
His promise is, I'll ne'er depart!

Where'er we walk, He's always there!
Our hand to hold, our joys to share,
His love unbounded knows no end;
Whate'er we need He'll freely send.

He dries our tears and makes us smile,
He lifts our hearts, whate'er the trial;
Like lightning, angels to our side,
Fly for our help, with us abide.

Who walks with Jesus, walks with God!
And treads the path that He has trod;
Abiding in the Father's love,
And fitted for a home above!

We soon shall in the glory be,
In mansions fair, God's family!
Rejoicing with the angel host;
With Father, Son and Holy Ghost!

Peace of heart and of mind are priceless. But how can I find peace in such a restless world? In the verses quoted below the Bible draws our attention to two truths. The first is that there cannot be any peace to men and women who live their lives without reference to God. And the second truth assures us that a peace which is beyond human understanding can be ours in whatever circumstances we may find ourselves. These verses express those truths.

"There is no peace, says the Lord, unto the wicked." Isaiah 48:22
"And the peace of God, which passes all understanding, shall keep your hearts and minds through Christ Jesus." Philippians 4:7

christian verse
for meditation

Bible references:
John 14:25-31
Colossians 3:15-17

PEACE

The restless world around us sighs,
And peace, like shadow quickly flies;
But men, who seek a place to hide,
Find peace close by the Saviour's side.

There is no peace, my God has said,
For wicked men, when truth has fled;
Like troubled sea, that cannot rest,
They seek for peace but are unblest.

The troubled sea, God's word declares,
Upon it's waves just dirt it bears,
Like all mankind, so lost in sin,
No peace it finds, no, none within.

But hear! the gospel's gracious sound,
Tells lost mankind peace can be found!
That Jesus is Himself our Peace,
For all who trust and do believe.

This Jesus is the King of Peace,
For He has borne sin's dread disease;
So, restless soul, take now your rest,
In Jesus' arms and on His breast.

Dear friend, this King invites us all,
To seek His face and on Him call:
So go to Him and take His rest,
Your King of Peace, a gracious guest!

Psalm 133 tells us how important fellowship is to the Christian believer. What is fellowship? It is the expression of that unity we all have in Jesus Christ. We are one Body, members one of another, with our head being the Lord himself. We are clothed in the same righteousness and all are cleansed from sin in His precious blood.

This fellowship is not something superficial, it is of the heart and spiritual. It centres on Christ and rejoices in Him. It also rejoices God Himself for this psalm tells us that where it exists He commands His blessing to fall upon such people. "For there the Lord commanded the blessing, even life for evermore."

Furthermore, true Christian fellowship transcends all barriers of class and nationality. In Christ we are all one. We have all been brought into fellowship with Jesus Christ and are therefore united to each other through Him.

christian verse
for meditation

FELLOWSHIP

How precious is the tie that binds
Believers to each other,
It is the oil poured from on high
From Him who is our Brother.

It makes us one, in Christian love,
It binds us all together,
We share our joys, and sorrows too,
And taste of heaven's measure.

How good, and, O, so pleasant too,
To dwell in harmony:
God's blessings, saints will surely prove
Who seek this unity.

The blessing there, does God appoint
And sends the Spirit down,
His saints He does with oil anoint,
With joy, He does them crown!

So, then, dear saints, let us be true
And run this race together,
We shall not fail, though we be few,
With God our heavenly Father.

FAITH AND HOPE

The poetry in this last section describes the great principle of the Christian life, namely the life of faith.

The Bible tells us in many places that we walk by faith and not by sight in the Christian pathway. The believer trusts in a Saviour that he or she has never seen with their eyes. And yet, Jesus is as real as He was to those who lived with Him when He was upon this earth.

Faith is trust. We trust in God on the basis of the bare word that He has spoken and which is recorded for us in the Bible.

With faith goes hope. The Christian hope is not something that may or may not happen. The Christian hope is a certainty because it is based on God's promises. And God cannot lie. To trust God on the bare word that He has spoken is to honour Him as trustworthy. To doubt His word is to question His truthfulness and therefore to dishonour Him.

To have faith is not to throw reason out of the window. Faith goes beyond reason. It goes where reason cannot go.

A great French genius and christian, Pascal, spoke of reason over against faith when he said, "Faith has its reasons which reason cannot know."

Faith is a gift of God. It is the eye of the soul and enables even the youngest child who is a Christian to know spiritual truth that the most learned non-christian can never know.

These poems speak of faith and the blessings that faith brings to all that put their trust in Jesus Christ.

What is it that you most desire? In the Bible we find that what the godly men of earlier ages desired most was to see the face of God. Within every human heart there is this sense, a longing, to be loved and wanted by someone who is bigger than ourselves. Only God can satisfy that desire. To see Him is to know that He loves us. In heaven we shall see the smile of His face and be filled with rapture and joy, as the prophet Isaiah tells us in this verse:-

"Your eyes will see the King in his beauty and view a land that stretches far." Isaiah 33:17

christian verse
for meditation

Bible references:
Isaiah 6:1-7
Luke 5:1-11

WE SHALL SEE GOD

Your eyes will see the King,
His beauty, crowned with grace:
Around His throne the saints all sing,
And see His lovely face!

The angels see that face,
It's radiance like the sun,
And with the saints their anthems raise
To heaven's beloved One.

What glory we shall see,
When heaven we enter in!
Made free by Christ, made clean and free,
Delivered from all sin!

The saints who've gone before,
And loved ones now above,
Will praise Him as we upward soar,
Embracing us in love!

And in that royal place,
United with the Lord,
Our praise will never, never, cease
As Jesus is adored!

Has true and lasting happiness eluded you in life? Our pursuit of happiness invariably leads to disappointment. Why is this? We need to understand that God has joined holiness and happiness together. They are two sides of the same coin. The Bible tells us that to be truly happy and blessed in this world we must walk in ways that please God. Psalm 119, the longest of the psalms, is all about this. The happy man is the blessed man. You cannot be happy unless holy, the writer of the psalm tells us.

"Happy are the people whose God is the Lord!" Psalm 144:15

christian verse
for meditation

THE HAPPY MAN

How blessed is he who walks with God,
Whose paths are undefiled;
No fear shall make his heart to fail,
Nor cause his feet to slide.

That man is blessed who loves God's law,
Whose soul delights therein;
Within his heart he keeps that word
So that he might not sin.

His soul, it swells with great desire,
It loves God's word alone,
For wondrous light breaks forth as he
Does meditate thereon.

Man's soul, without God's word, it will
Seek only things external,
But quickened by the Spirit's breath
He seeks for things internal.

The upright heart will praise our God,
For righteous judgments true:
The soul that learns those paths to choose,
With joy God will endue.

O thou my God, teach me Your ways,
To understand Your paths,
So shall I praise Your wondrous Name,
And worship fill my heart.

The great question facing us all is what happens after death. When we were young perhaps this did not overmuch concern us. But as we get older the reality of the great issues of life and death confront us more urgently. A great man, who lived many centuries ago, Job, faced this question. Being a man who believed God, he was given assurance that all would be well. This man of faith uttered these timeless words which will give all believers great assurance that they, too, will stand in resurrected and glorified bodies, and with great joy see God.

"I know that my Redeemer lives, and that in the end he will stand upon the earth. And after my skin has been destroyed, yet in my flesh I shall see God; I myself will see him with my own eyes - I, and not another." Job 19.25-27

christian verse
for meditation

RESURRECTION ASSURED

Shall I see God with open eyes,
When my poor soul flies to the skies?
Yes, I shall see Him, face to face,
When I have run this earthly race.

What joy is this that I should rise,
Ascend on high into the skies!
For there will I, through Jesus' blood
Stand in pure light and see my God!

Yes, I myself, will walk on high
With all the angels in the sky,
And with them there my song will be -
Just see what God has done for me!

So, fearful soul, trust in your God,
And lift your eyes to Him above,
For there in heaven your Saviour waits
To greet you at its open gates!

The Bible tells us that faith is the gift of God. It is by grace, through faith in Jesus and His finished work on the cross, that we are saved. And it is by faith that we continue to walk in this world until faith gives way to sight in the world to which we are going.

"For by grace are you saved, through faith, and that not of yourselves, it is the gift of God". Ephesians 2.8

christian verse
for meditation

Bible references:
Matthew 9:18-38
Matthew 17:14-21

FAITH

We walk by faith, and not by sight,
It is the way that God has planned;
By faith we see the promise bright
And walk secure, safe in His hand.

The path that God appoints for us,
Oft times is dark, and lonely too,
Our Father's heart, a heart of love,
Has planned that path for me and you.

He calls us all to trust Him still,
The future's His, not ours to say,
And then we find His perfect will
Is joy indeed upon the Way.

To walk by faith, and not by sight,
Our nature finds this hard to bear,
But faith alone breaks through the night
To show our Jesus standing there.

'Tis faith that mounts to starry skies
To see the One enthroned above,
Beyond the sight of worldly eyes,
The sinners Friend whose name is Love.

This faith takes hold of Jesus' hands,
The hands that cruel nails did pierce,
Kind hands which keep the stars in place,
And hold us in a warm embrace.

This faith alone, it pleases God,
A gift of grace through Jesus' blood;
So reach and take this precious gift,
So freely given that you might live.

The love of God is demonstrated supremely in the sacrifice of Jesus for our sins. God is angry with sin and His wrath rests upon sinners until they come to Jesus in repentance and faith. It is not God's will that any should perish but that all should come to a knowledge of salvation. For God did not send His Son into the world to condemn the world, but to save the world through him. Whoever believes in him is not condemned. This is a great cause for rejoicing and gladness as we rest our souls on him.

"In returning and in rest shall you be saved; in quietness and in confidence shall be your strength." Isaiah 30:15

christian verse
for meditation

Bible references:
Matthew 11:25-30
John 14:15-31
Philippians 4:4-7

THE SAINT'S REST

In quietness and confidence
Rest in your God alone;
Join angels in His presence
And worship at His throne.

Dear, troubled, soul look there and see
Your Saviour and your Friend,
His cross and sufferings set you free
When at His feet you bend.

This God and Saviour took your sins
And bore them to the tree,
In love and sorrow paid the price,
To make you clean and free.

He made your sorrows and your griefs
To be His very own:
He took them to a place far off,
No more shall they be known.

In that far place your sins are hid
Remembered there no more:
For love of your poor soul this did
That you may grace adore.

With joy and gladness I will sing
Of One so kind and good,
Who loved me when I loved Him not,
And shed for me His blood.

All praise and honour be to Him
Who rules in heaven above;
And may I ever sing His praise
Who fills my heart with love.

Where do you turn to when you are in any kind of trouble? Of course, we naturally turn to loved ones or to close friends who will show us understanding and give us advice. But what if we do not have anyone to turn to, or if our problem is beyond the help of a fellow human being? The Bible tells us that Jesus is a friend who stays closer to us than a brother! We see, again and again, illustrations in the Bible of men and women who have turned to God in their distress and found Him a very present help in time of trouble. The psalmist was a case in point as this verse tells us.

"In my distress I called to the Lord; I cried to my God for help. From His temple He heard my voice; my cry came before Him, into His ears." Psalm 16:6

christian verse
for meditation

Bible references:
John 15:9-17
Revelation 21:1-5
Revelation 22:1-7

GOD IS MY FRIEND

In my distress I called to You,
My God, my dearest Friend,
And quickly to my aid You came
To help and to defend.

You caused your face to smile upon
My troubled mind and heart,
And in those beams of love divine
My fears did fast depart.

My feet, like hinds feet, You did make,
And caused me sure to stand,
And leap for joy when all around
Was dark and sinking sand.

I praise you Lord, so faithfully
You speed to our relief;
You hear our cries and see our tears,
Then take away our grief.

What blessings fall upon our heads
From a dear Father's heart;
We praise and bless You, O our God,
That this should be our part!

We praise You, too, that Jesus died,
And bore our sins and griefs,
That we may share in all your joys;
Within have perfect peace!

The people of God, from the very beginning, have looked forward to the coming of Jesus into the world. The Old Testament scriptures have many prophecies concerning His coming and God's people held on to those promises as their great hope for the future. They spoke of the "hope of His coming" with great joy. Only Jesus Christ gives us hope for time and for eternity for He holds the keys of the future. In Him alone we have hope and, ultimately, the hope of everlasting life in heaven through faith in His blood which He shed for us when He died for our sins on the cross.

"Blessed is the man who trusts in the Lord, and whose hope is the Lord. For he shall be like a tree planted by the waters, which spreads out its roots by the river, and will not fear when heat comes; but its leaf will be green, and will not be anxious in the year of drought, nor will cease from yielding fruit.! Jeremiah 17:7,8

"Now may the God of hope fill you with all joy and peace in believing, that you may abound in hope...." Romans 15:13

christian verse
for meditation

Bible references:
Psalm 62
Psalm 147
Titus 2:11-14

THE SINNER'S HOPE

O God of glory, God of grace,
What joy to see your lovely face,
Revealed in Jesus, your dear Son,
Who came to earth, our race to run.

In Bethlehem's stall the babe was laid,
Born of Mary, a Hebrew maid;
Adored by angels, shepherds too,
This child in favour daily grew.

They called him Jesus, blessed Name,
The sinner's hope, for such he came;
He walked this earth in love and grace
To reach and save our fallen race.

A bruiséd reed he will not break,
But heal that soul for his Name's sake,
Nor will he quench the smoking flax
But pour on oil which now it lacks.

His love is boundless, always free,
Like sunshine, covers land and sea;
A love that will not let you go,
When brought by grace that love to know.

And so, dear soul, your certain hope,
Rests in this Man who low did stoop;
He'll walk with you through life's short day
And then in heaven forever stay.

Who are we and why are we here in this world? These are
questions that many people ask and yet few find a satisfactory
answer. The Bible alone gives us that answer. It tells us that we
came from the hand of God and that we shall go back to God when
we die. It tells us, too, that this creation was made for man to rule
and to enjoy. The history of man is a history of tragedy through Satan
tempting man to sin and so ruin the Paradise that God had made.
But the wonder is that Jesus came to restore that which had
been lost through Adam's folly.

*"Then the Lord God took the man (Adam) and put him in the
garden of Eden to tend and keep it". Genesis 2:15*

christian verse
for meditation

Bible references:
Genesis chapter 3
John 1:1-18
2Peter 3:1-13
Revelation 21:22-27

GOD'S ETERNAL PURPOSE FOR MAN

All praise to Him who rules on high,
Our God whose fingers made the sky;
His love and bounty knows no bounds,
All heaven His praise and worship sounds.

He made the stars and moon and sun,
He spoke, creation's work was done!
At His command the darkness fled
And light eternal shone instead.

And on creation's stage, His plan
For there to rule a perfect man;
So Adam from the dust was made,
In wonder stood and all surveyed.

What sights there met his wondering eyes!
As with his God beneath the skies,
He viewed his home that knew no sin,
A Paradise made just for him.

But from afar there rose a cloud,
A fallen angel, O so proud!
Lucifer, now moved with hate
To ruin man, to share his fate.

And there, in that fair Paradise,
The Evil One fast spread his lies,
So tempted man to heed his voice,
And foolishly make death his choice.

All nature cried, as Adam fell,
Forsaking bliss and choosing hell,
And angels wept as they surveyed
The ruined world that God had made.

But little did that traitor know,
The woman's Seed would overthrow
That Wicked One upon the cross,
And for our sakes there suffer loss!

In love and mercy for our race
God sent His Son to take our place,
And there upon the cross (dread day),
A sacrifice, sin's price to pay.

For God so loved the human race,
(For all His thoughts are thoughts of grace),
He freely gave, that we might live,
The greatest gift that He could give.

Now Jesus reigns o'er all supreme
Above all empires, worlds unseen;
To Him all power has now been given
On earth beneath, above in heaven.

This ruined world He will remake;
So fallen man, his hand now takes,
To lead him up to worlds on high,
Where He has mansions in the sky.

Look up, you saints, from this lost world,
And see the bliss God will unfold;
For all His children, saved by grace,
Will see the beauty of His face!

Faith has been described as the "eye of the soul". Faith reaches where reason cannot go. With our human reason we cannot discover or know God. But with faith we can know Him and in knowing Him we learn to love Him. These verses demonstrate that faith is superior to sight when it comes to spiritual things. The smallest child with true faith can know things that an unbeliever, however intelligent, can never know.

"But without faith it is impossible to please God, for he who comes to Him must believe that He is, and that He is a rewarder of those who diligently seek Him." Hebrews 11:6

christian verse
for meditation

Bible references:
I Corinthians 1:18-30
Hebrews 11:1-3

THE FAITH THAT SEES GOD

We walk by faith and not by sight.
Through brightest day and darkest night;
Though unperceived by mortal sense
Our Saviour is our sure defence.

By faith, we see what human eyes
Cannot perceive beyond the skies;
This faith, it sees the throne of God
A throne of grace through Jesus' blood!

Such faith can reach where sight must fail.
It goes within the holy veil!
The veil which hides a holy God
Now opened up through Jesus' blood.

The greatest mind must surely fail
To enter through that holy veil;
Mere reason is too frail to know
A holy God from earth below.

By wisdom, God did so ordain
That man's poor reason will not gain
A sight of Him who dwells in light
Amidst the fire of awesome sight.

So friend, now cease to pit your mind
Against our God who rules mankind;
Submit your will, and now repent
And take the gift of faith He's sent.

The spiritual world can only be seen and appreciated through the eye of faith. Our earthly senses can only take us so far. They cannot enter into divine mysteries which are only revealed to faith. The patriarch, Job, asked the timeless question, Canst thou by searching find out God? This was a rhetorical question for it emphasizes the inability of man to discover God with his natural faculties. The scripture verse below tells us that we cannot discover the truth of God unaided but, rather, it is revealed to us by the Holy Spirit. By faith we apprehend what God has revealed, not by reason. The mathematician and genius, Pascal, said, Faith has it's reasons which reason cannot know!

"Eye has not seen, nor ear heard, neither has entered into the heart of man, the things that God has prepared for them that love Him but God has revealed it to us by His Spirit." I Corinthians 2:9

christian verse
for meditation

Bible references:
Job chapters 11 and 12
John chapter 10
1 Corinthians chapter 2

BY FAITH

The Christian needs no earthly light,
He walks by faith and not by sight,
His eyes are fixed on heaven above
Where Jesus reigns, our God of love.

His earthly senses he disdains,
They cannot reach where Jesus reigns,
By faith he sees God's throne on high,
It's glories hid from mortal eye!

In that place where Jesus is,
No storms can reach and all is peace,
The troubled saint there finds his rest,
In Jesus' arms, against His breast.

Safe in that place from Satan's darts,
From hell's fierce face and scowl so dark,
The Christian looks to Christ alone,
Who intercedes for all His own.

Our great high priest in heaven above,
Has entered in with His own blood,
The blood that cleanses from all sin,
And welcomes guilty sinners in!

Above the portal of the door*
He reads the words of welcome, sure,
That God has opened this new way
And bids us come without delay!

This door is never closed to those
Who plead the merit of His blood,
For there they see a Father's face,
And arms outstretched in
matchless grace!

*The "portal of the door" refers to the door lintel
which was sprinkled with blood by the Israelites on
the night that they were delivered from Egyptian
bondage. The destroying angel saw the blood and
passed over them. Hence the meaning of the word
"Passover" (see Exodus chapter 12). So, Jesus has, by
His blood, made peace with God for us, thus
ensuring a welcome by the Father.

A birthday anniversary is a good time for reflection, as is any anniversary. If we review our lives we will be surprised at the many blessings that have come our way, even though there may well have been tearful times and sadnesses. The Bible tells us that God works all things together for good for those who love Him, and that, though we cannot know what the future holds for us we know that a loving heavenly Father is in control of our destiny so all things will have a happy outcome, of that we can be certain. It is a comfort to know that our Saviour, Jesus Christ, knows exactly what it is like to live in this world. In heaven is One who knew the joys and the sorrows that are part and parcel of this earthly life and therefore can sympathise with us in our distresses and enter into our joys too.

"And we know that all things work together for good to those who love God, to those who are the called according to His purpose."
Romans 8:28

A BIRTHDAY

Each year on year, your God on high
Has ever kept His loving eye
Upon you, His beloved one,
For whom He gave His only Son!

In faith you've walked down through these years,
The laughter sometimes mixed with tears,
But Jesus knows the way you take,
For here He walked, all for your sake!

And now in heaven, prepares a place,
A mansion built with stones of grace!
A home where joy and love abound,
Nor sin, nor tears, can e'er be found!

And so, dear saint, lift up your head,
For paths of joy your feet will tread!
See Jesus, smiling, beckoning on
And in His hand the crown you've won!

New paths, new joys, will yet unfold,
With blessings that cannot be told,
For Jesus works all things for good,
Who freely shed His precious blood!

All things, He'll give, who freely gave
His only Son, your soul to save!
Reach out in faith and take His hand,
Each day will show what He has planned!

All praise to God who lives on high,
Who paints the stars seen in the sky,
Whose hand, so strong, now reaches down
To bless your years and mercies crown!

Notes